Over the years I have had the honor not only to participate in the Brooklyn Tabernacle's services but to enjoy the kindness, inspiring friendship, and love of the Cymbalas. They are a unique family. I wholeheartedly commend their daughter Chrissy for her courage and desire to share her tender and difficult story. Yet, as she writes, it is not really her story—but rather God's story. He is the Grand Weaver who knows our frayed threads that we seek to hide and unravel, which He alone is able to knit together into a beautiful tapestry as we surrender to Him. I believe you will be both touched and challenged by her deeply moving book. I truly believe it can be a life changer for many.

DR. RAVI ZACHARIAS
Author and speaker

In *Girl in the Song*, Chrissy Cymbala Toledo engages us with a transformative truth: The purpose of God is greater than the brokenness of man. As her journey depicts, God does great things with broken pieces.

REV. DR. SAMUEL RODRIGUEZ
President, NHCLC/Conela Hispanic Evangelical Association

Beautiful girl, beautiful story! I respect Chrissy's parents, Jim and Carol, and I wholeheartedly believe in the power of prayer and good parents. I am so proud of Chrissy, and I believe that many ministers should tune in to how their kids view God and the church!

NICKY CRUZ
Evangelist and author of *Run, Baby, Run*

An amazing tale of redemption and light breaking through darkness. Chrissy Cymbala Toledo's story of spiritual transformation is an inspiration to us all.

DR. ROBERT JEFFRESS
Senior pastor, First Baptist Church, Dallas, TX

Girl in the Song is a book for anyone who has ever yearned for true love and acceptance. As you experience the music God is writing through Chrissy's story and yours, you'll sense His hand on your own life and draw closer to His heart.

LIONEL HOLLINS
Head coach, Brooklyn Nets

Girl in the Song offers much-needed hope and encouragement. It's the story of what happens when God moves people to pray. It's a story of redemption, grace, and love. Chrissy's journey will bless you, and in the process, God may prompt you to get another copy for someone else who has lost their way.

MICHAEL CATT
Senior pastor, Sherwood Baptist Church, and executive producer, Sherwood Pictures

A compelling, must-read story that will touch your heart. With beauty and vulnerability, Chrissy Cymbala Toledo shares what it means to be lost and found again, and how the power of grace can redeem any situation.

DARLENE ZSCHECH
Senior pastor, Hope Unlimited Church

We all have chapters in our lives we'd rather not disclose. Everybody has to contend with his or her own personal version of a sinful heart. Everybody. Chrissy Toledo combines great courage and humble transparency in sharing her story. She offers hope to people who want to exchange theirs for a new heart from God.

PAUL WESTPHAL
Assistant coach, Brooklyn Nets

In this book Chrissy Cymbala Toledo details her "run away from God" days and the faithful love of her parents. They never gave up and neither did the church! Chrissy found her way back and now she and her husband have been instrumental in helping to lead a spiritual turnaround for thousands of people. All of us find a piece of ourselves in Chrissy's story.

RICH WILKERSON SR.
Lead pastor, TrinityChurch.TV, Miami, FL

Intimate and emotionally compelling, *Girl in the Song* is the page-turning story of one woman's journey to discover her true self—and the God who loved her through it all.

DR. TONY EVANS
Senior pastor, Oak Cliff Bible Fellowship, and president,
The Urban Alternative

To
Anne
From
Morag
with love + many blessings X

GIRL IN THE SONG

GIRL
IN THE
SONG

THE TRUE STORY
*of a young woman who lost her way—
and the miracle that led her home*

CHRISSY CYMBALA TOLEDO

**TYNDALE®
MOMENTUM**

*An Imprint of
Tyndale House Publishers, Inc.*

Visit Tyndale online at www.tyndale.com.

Visit Tyndale Momentum online at www.tyndalemomentum.com.

Tyndale Momentum and the Tyndale Momentum logo are registered trademarks of Tyndale House Publishers, Inc. Tyndale Momentum is an imprint of Tyndale House Publishers, Inc., Carol Stream, Illinois.

Girl in the Song: The True Story of a Young Woman Who Lost Her Way—and the Miracle That Led Her Home

Designed by Jennifer Ghionzoli

Edited by Bonne Steffen

Published in association with the literary agency of Ann Spangler and Company, 1415 Laurel Avenue, SE, Grand Rapids, MI 49506.

Unless otherwise indicated, all Scripture quotations are taken from the *Holy Bible*, King James Version.

Scripture quotations marked NLT are taken from the *Holy Bible*, New Living Translation, copyright © 1996, 2004, 2007, 2013 by Tyndale House Foundation. Used by permission of Tyndale House Publishers, Inc., Carol Stream, Illinois 60188. All rights reserved.

Some names have been changed for the privacy of the individuals involved.

Library of Congress Cataloging-in-Publication Data

Toledo, Chrissy Cymbala.
  Girl in the song : the true story of a young woman who lost her way—and the miracle that led her home / Chrissy Cymbala Toledo.
    pages cm
  Includes bibliographical references.
  ISBN 978-1-4143-7863-3 (sc : alk. paper)   1. Toledo, Chrissy Cymbala.   2. Christian biography—United States.   I. Title.
  BR1725.T58A3 2015
  277.3'083092—dc23
  [B]   2015013279

Printed in the United States of America

21   20   19   18   17   16   15
7   6   5   4   3   2   1

Dedicated to my husband,
a selfless man who lives to secure the blessing for others

FOREWORD

EVERY LIFE HAS ITS SHARE OF TWISTS AND TURNS. I was a young businessman working for an airline company, newly married with my first child, when I answered the call to full-time ministry. With neither formal training nor ministry experience, my wife Carol and I took over a struggling church in downtown Brooklyn. For the next twenty years we spent our lives helping people, many of whom were ravaged by pain and bound by inner turmoil.

How that pain surfaces in the midst of life's emotional storms can often be ugly and difficult to deal with. Though it felt like an uphill struggle, we soon began to see remarkable breakthroughs as people's lives were transformed by the power of Jesus. Witnessing such changes encouraged us to keep going.

In the midst of helping others, we were taken by surprise the moment a chaotic storm engulfed our own family. Though I touched on my experience with our daughter Chrissy in my book *Fresh Wind, Fresh Fire*, I didn't feel at liberty to disclose everything that occurred during those tumultuous years.

What you are about to read is Chrissy's story, a behind-the-scenes look at a young girl who was surrounded by people who loved her, yet fell prey to influences that threatened to tear her apart.

As a pastor, I would like to encourage anyone who wonders whether there is something more to life than the latest relationship to open her heart as she reads the story Chrissy has to tell. As a father, I want to urge parents who are tempted to lose hope for a child to read Chrissy's story before concluding there are limits to what God can do.

Whatever your situation, whether it is hard or easy right now, I hope *Girl in the Song* will help you face life's storms in ways that will bring you peace and make you strong.

Pastor Jim Cymbala
Brooklyn Tabernacle

PROLOGUE

I DIDN'T WANT TO LOOK IN THE MIRROR—I loathed the person who stared back. She was selfish and ungrateful and had blown it over and over again. Her decisions over these past years had created a deep crevasse between her and the people who loved her.

Will there ever be peace between us again? I wondered. As I hurried to finish in the bathroom and get ready for bed, I tried to forget what had happened with my parents. There were moments when I could push it all out of my mind, but then I would be squeezed by such loneliness that I wanted to cry out.

I was certainly grateful for one thing—I had a safe place to live, a generous offer from a dear friend. Before leaving this evening, Lorna had made sure I had everything I needed, mentioning that there was plenty of food in the kitchen. The house was so quiet without her lively personality filling the rooms.

I lay in bed, trying to sleep, but my emotions wouldn't let me, cresting and plunging like a roller coaster. When I finally closed my eyes, it seemed that something changed in the room, but I couldn't say exactly what. I reopened my eyes and glanced around to my right, my left . . . and then there, at the foot of the bed, I spied something shadowy. It didn't have a body like a person or any facial features that I could make out. Standing there in the bedroom, the shape was so much blacker than the darkness of the room that it was visible. I sensed it was looking at me.

I didn't know what was going to happen next. My life had once been wonderful, with so much to look forward to. How had things gone so terribly wrong?

CHAPTER

1

IT WAS 9 P.M. and I looked up at my dad as we walked down a dark, dismal block of Atlantic Avenue in Brooklyn, New York. Even at four years old, I noticed that he looked much different from most of the people we passed—Dad was clean-shaven, well dressed, with nice-smelling cologne. I was oblivious to the sadness that surrounded me.

"Daddy, wait a minute. One of my shoes got unbuckled."

My dad apprehensively let my hand go but didn't take his eyes off of me, not even for a second. I bent down over my dark blue kneesocks, smiling as I reached for my shoes. They were bright red, and they were my favorite thing, more important than any doll or toy I had. I took my time buckling the strap, admiring the shoes for just a bit too long.

Dad gently pulled me by the hand. "Ready?"

"Yes, Daddy, I did it myself. See?"

We continued down the street, and I giggled as he squeezed my hand three times. It was our secret way of saying I. LOVE. YOU. I would squeeze his hand three times too. Back and forth, back and forth, we'd talk in our special code. The concrete pavement was cracked and bumpy under my feet, and I made a game out of trying not to step on the cracks.

The rumbling sound of the subway under my red shoes was, in part, the music of the streets. A strong burst of air whooshed up through the grate as a train passed underground, blowing my fine blonde hair over my eyes. Dad gently swept my hair off my face so that I could see.

At that moment, I caught a whiff of the odor that always made me wrinkle my nose. I didn't know that the pungent smell was mostly from urine. I didn't think much about why there was loose, smelly garbage on the sidewalk. I just made sure I didn't step on anything. The sights and sounds of the city were just an indication to me that we were close . . . close to the center of my world.

I looked across the street and saw the lady who always stood in the same place under the streetlight. She wore lots of makeup and sparkly clothes and was always talking to a man through the window of his car. When I turned to look back and saw her get into the car, I wondered, *Where is she always going?*

Before I could ask my dad, someone shouted from farther down the block. I recognized his voice right away, but I couldn't understand what he was saying.

"Oh no, Daddy, *he's* waiting for you again!"

We continued down the street, and I pulled on Dad's arm. "What do you think he wants tonight, Daddy?"

As we got closer, I could see the man struggling to get up from the cardboard mat that was sliding underneath him.

"Father, Father!" he shouted, his words seeming to mush together.

He had a bottle clutched tightly in one hand while he tried to raise the other, hoping to get my dad's attention

Father? I thought.

"Daddy, *you're* not his father!" I exclaimed.

He looked at me and just smiled.

Kneeling down next to the man, Dad laughed and said, "I'm a pastor, not a priest." Even though it wasn't cold out, the man was shaking. Daddy talked quietly to him. "Hey, my friend, you're not looking so good tonight."

Dad's blue eyes filled with tenderness met the man's bloodshot gaze. He reached over and touched the man's shoulder, which I thought looked really dirty.

"Would you come see me in the morning?"

The man didn't respond. Instead, he laid his head back down on his paper bag pillow, holding the empty bottle to his chest. I could see that Daddy was really sad, and it made me sad too. He was kind to everyone, especially people that others wanted to hurry by. Dad always looked at hurting people with so much love in his eyes. Maybe it was because he grew up in a home watching his own father's hands tremble.

"Come here, Chrissy," Grandpa would say with his arms out, unable to keep from shaking because of his drunkenness.

I never wanted to be near Grandpa, and I surely didn't want

to give him a hug. I cringed when he would set me on his knee, trying to still himself enough to talk to me. He would lean his face close to mine, and I would squirm and turn my head away because I didn't like the smell of his breath.

"Grandma, where are you?" I would call out, hoping she would come get me. But my attempt at a rescue only seemed to make Grandpa hold me tighter.

No matter what Grandpa said or did, Grandma's response was always caring and considerate. When he raised his voice, she would answer him quietly. Year after year, she saw beyond what things were and believed that change would come. What I didn't know at that age was that sometimes Grandma had to call my dad in the middle of the night because Grandpa had struck her and she was hurt badly. My dad had grown up living with an abusive father and watching his mother endure through the hardest times without becoming bitter. Even though she had every reason to leave Grandpa, she never did.

As an escape from the turmoil at home, Dad spent the majority of his days on some of the worst playgrounds in the city because that's where the best basketball was. Playing ball in the fifties, he quickly learned how to get along with all kinds of people and ended up creating a whole new world outside of his home. Little did he know that he was being shaped to have a heart for the people in the neighborhood that his little church would be in one day.

It looked to me as though the man on the ground had fallen asleep, so I tugged at Dad's sleeve. He slowly stepped away and pulled keys out of his pocket. The dim light above the sign that read Brooklyn Gospel Tabernacle cast a long shadow on the sidewalk that I loved to step on. *Click, click* . . . the first and second locks opened and Dad switched on the light. I reached down to scoop up the scattered envelopes that had been pushed through the slot in the door.

"I've got the mail, Daddy!" I said and ran up the stairs, leaving him behind.

"I'll turn on the lights in your office, too!" I shouted through the railing.

Running my hands along the faded light blue walls, I inhaled the mouthwatering aroma that lingered from dinners that had been cooked that night in the apartments above our small church sanctuary. I loved those meals just as much as the ones Mom made for us. One of the tenants, Rina, was Filipino and made egg rolls, and the Ali family, who were from Trinidad, ate delicious roti stuffed with curried chicken. I reached the second floor, wondering who might be awake.

Skipping loudly through the hallway and into Dad's office, I was hoping someone would peek out of an apartment door and notice I was there. I flipped on the light switch, set the mail on my dad's desk, then plopped onto the green vinyl chair against the paneled wall, noticing that my red shoes were a bit scuffed from skipping on the sidewalk.

When Dad came in, he dropped our overnight bags on the floor and sat in his desk chair, shuffling through the pile of envelopes. For whatever reason, he always looked worried when he opened the mail. I licked my fingers and was trying to rub the scuff marks off my shoes when the picture hanging on the wall caught my attention, just as it always did.

It was a painting of Jesus standing next to a building as tall as a skyscraper. Jesus was as big as the building and was knocking on the windows. I had talked about it several times with Dad.

"Daddy, that looks like Jesus knocking on a building in New York."

"It does. Jesus really cares for the people in this city," he said, opening one envelope after another.

My gaze wandered from the painting to Dad. I loved him so much, and he made me feel so special when I was with him. I never wanted to be anywhere but by his side.

"Where's my *lee-tal* girl?" I heard Rina call out in her heavy Filipino accent from the apartment down the hall.

"Rina!" I jumped up from my chair and ran out to greet her. Wrapping my arms around her hips, I hugged her tightly as she pulled me into her kitchen.

"Come in, I will give you some snacks." Barely five feet tall, she wore a floral print housedress and slippers, and her thick dark brown hair was tied up in a bun. As usual, her kitchen counter was filled with cookies and other treats she'd bought in Chinatown.

"Ooh, can I have some pineapple juice with my cookies, Rina?"

"Of course, my leetal princess," she answered.

Rina and her husband always kept a guest room ready for us, with a bed for Dad to sleep in as well as a makeshift bed for me on the floor. I loved staying overnight at Rina's when Dad decided to work late because it was such an adventure. I would run all over the building, exploring every corner. And even better, I got to be with Rina, a person I adored.

I finished up my snacks, changed into my cozy pajamas, and lay down on the fluffy blanket that was spread out on the worn shag carpet. Rina shuffled into the room and kissed me good-night, turning off the lights so that I could settle in. I lay there in the dark listening to the noise coming through the slightly opened window—far-off sirens, honking horns, and blaring music blended together, sounding like a crazy song. Starting to doze off, I heard laughter—Rina and her husband were talking in the kitchen. I loved my world.

As I slept, Dad would usually work late, sitting alone in his office down the hall. The reality of what he faced every day as the pastor of this church must have crowded his mind. The problems seemed somehow veiled when I was with him—his distraction, a four-year-old girl who loved being with her daddy. But now, in the stillness, pangs of doubt must have entered his thoughts. It had been almost a year since he'd resigned from a promising career at American Airlines to take this church in an area where heroin was as easy to buy as a carton of milk.

There was absolutely nothing appealing about the neighborhood or the building that might draw people to this place. The Brooklyn Tabernacle was not in a good situation. Collections taken on Sundays were sometimes stolen before they could be counted and the few people who attended could barely support themselves, let alone a struggling church. The wood-like paneled walls of that second floor office must have felt like they were closing in on Dad that night. To me this was an adventure; not so for him.

Suddenly on this night I woke up, startled by screaming

sirens speeding by the building. I looked toward the empty guest bed. *Where's Daddy?* I got up and tiptoed through the kitchen, then out into the hallway. A small light shone from the office, the door slightly ajar. I quietly approached, peeked through the opening, and saw something that was not unusual to me. Dad was praying. But he was not just praying . . . he was listening. Even as a little girl, I knew that's what he was doing because his eyes were closed and his face looked like someone who was looking at something beautiful.

CHAPTER

2

THE NEXT MORNING WAS CRISP AND COOL, a breeze catching the scent of Rina's breakfast on the stove, wafting it my way. Jumping up, I grabbed the blanket from the floor and wrapped it around me.

"Leetal girl, do I hear you up?"

"Yes, coming!" I spotted a pair of her shoes and quickly stepped into them, half tripping, half dragging my feet to the kitchen.

"It's almost ten o'clock, and your daddy's ready to go. I will feed you and get you ready," Rina said. I glanced out into the hallway and heard my dad on the phone, the faint fragrance of his cologne still in the air. Rina had offered him coffee earlier, but he had already gone to the diner down the street for a cup of coffee to go—with lots of cream and sugar, just the way he liked it.

Although Dad would pray and study his Bible for hours a day, he didn't like to wait very long for things. That was why we spent the night at the church, so that he could avoid getting stuck in rush-hour traffic between New York and New Jersey. "Daddy, are we going through the tunnel again to get home?" I asked as we crossed the street toward our car.

"Yep, we are," he assured me. "But we need to get to Manhattan to go through the Holland Tunnel." The view as we drove over the Manhattan Bridge that day was amazing, with the skyline glistening in the late morning sun. You didn't have to wear seat belts in those days, so I knelt beside him and put my arm around his neck while we drove down the ramp onto Canal Street.

"Hey Chrissy, look over there," Dad said, pointing toward the other side of the street. I giggled at a Chinese man waving a large purplish squid in one hand and an even bigger red fish in his other hand while the crowd of customers pressed around him, elbowing each other, trying to snatch the delicacies. As we drove through the center of Chinatown, the streets became narrower, the buildings were closer, and the people seemed to be packed together like a box of crayons. Bright red and gold signs covered crowded storefronts, and the satin coats and scarves hanging outside reminded me of a beautiful rainbow.

As soon as Dad began to roll down the window, a strong stink flooded the car, making me squeeze my nostrils shut. Fish!

"I don't like fish, Daddy, especially the way Rina eats them with the eyeballs still in them!"

Dad laughed. "But what about what Lorna makes—Jamaican ackee and saltfish?"

"I like that, Daddy, 'cause there are no eyeballs!"

Jamaicans, Puerto Ricans, Filipinos—these were just some of the different cultures surrounding me as a little girl. My world was so exciting and fascinating because I had the advantage of growing up in a family that didn't see a person's color. I never thought about the fact that we were the only Caucasian family in our church. I simply learned how to love people by watching my parents.

"There's the tunnel, Chrissy." Dad began to slow down, merging into the single line of cars.

"I can do it, Daddy! Can I throw the change?" Going through the Holland Tunnel was like being on an amusement park ride for me.

"Okay, but remember: Aim for the middle." He held on to me while I reached across and tossed a quarter into the toll basket.

The music of the tunnel now began. The distinct sound of the cars' engines as they echoed off the walls was a new melody to my ears. I began to hear music everywhere, from the echoes in the tunnel, to the rumbling of the subway, to the rhythm of my footsteps on Rina's hardwood floors.

We drove another twenty minutes before arriving at our home in Maplewood, New Jersey. Our house was cozy and nicely furnished. Sometimes I thought about that man who lived on the street, sleeping outside our church. I wondered what he thought about his home, because I loved mine so much. Did he *like* sleeping on the sidewalk? Did he have a mommy and daddy like I did, and did they worry about him?

We parked in front of our small yellow house on a quiet,

tree-lined street. Dad opened the huge door of our brown sedan and I jumped out, dashing onto our large front yard. The springy grass looked like a green carpet under my feet, making me want to twirl until I got dizzy and fell to the ground. I lay there looking up at the clear blue sky, watching the birds fly back and forth, perching in the tall, sprawling trees.

I saw Mom looking for us from the big window in the living room, and soon she was at the door, smiling through the glass pane. I scrambled to my feet because I couldn't wait to be near her. She was beautiful. Her hair was thick and long, and when it wasn't flowing down her back, it was in a pretty bun on the top of her head. She was the picture of someone who was *warm* and *down to earth* and always made our home a comfortable, inviting place.

My mom was also really funny and often made us all laugh because she wasn't too proud to act silly. One time when my younger sister and I were disobeying her and being really naughty, Mom grabbed a broom and chased us around the dining table. She was having fun running after us. We weren't sure whether to laugh or cry!

She moved through life with a grace and ability to keep things light in the midst of the most pressure-filled times. No doubt it was one of the things that got our family through those early days in ministry. She could have struggled with the whole idea of her husband leaving his comfortable position in the business world for something that would require so much from them as a couple. She could have pressured my dad to give her the American dream after they were married. But she didn't. She had a sensitive heart to do what she felt *God* wanted her to do.

The adventure my family was on meant taking this church in Brooklyn, and Mom was all for it.

Besides the gift of laughter, Mom had another unique gift. She could play songs on the piano without any music in front of her. *Beautiful music.* While dinner was simmering on the stove, she would sit at the piano and turn single notes into elaborate chord progressions, naturally flowing from her fingertips.

"Chrissy, come here. I want to play something for you!" she called up to me one day while I was busy coloring in my room. The truth is, because I was always hearing music in my head, I was *always* tuned in to the songs she played, wherever I was. It was the special bond my mom and I had. When she was playing, I'd often sit on her lap and stare at her hands or hold her wrists as she touched the keys, pretending my hands were making hers move.

Now, as Mom's fingers moved effortlessly across the keys, she said, "C'mon, let's sing, too. 'O come, let us adore Him, O come, let us adore Him.'"

Mimicking her sweet tone, I sang along: "O come, let us adore Him, Christ, the Lord!" The song ended and she paused, then suddenly without warning, she started playing what sounded like circus music! "Christmas is almost here, and that means your birthday is almost here"! In the funniest of voices she began to sing, "Happy birthday to Chris, she's giving me a kiss, her mommy's so silly, hap-py birthday to Chris!"

She grabbed me and smothered my neck with kisses that tickled. Giggling, I begged, "Do it again, Mommy. Again!" And she would, over and over again, to my delight. Love and music permeated our home. When Mom wasn't working on a melody at the piano, she would be singing or playing a record album. My parents' collection was diverse in style, with one thing in common: All of the records had songs that moved the heart.

As Dad pulled our overnight bag out of the trunk, Mom opened the door. "Jim, hurry! I need to show you something!"

"Carol, just give me a second while I bring our things upstairs."

"No, please, Jim . . . come here—you won't believe this!" she exclaimed.

Dad and I followed her into the kitchen, where my mom pointed at the table. "Late last night, the doorbell rang," she began. "I ran down from our room wondering who would come to the house unannounced so late in the evening. When I opened the door nobody was there, but there were these four bags of groceries on the front steps. There wasn't a note or a car in front, nothing at all. Jim, it's everything we need for the next few weeks. It's a miracle!"

Mom paused, eagerly waiting for my dad to say something. I was surprised when he hung his head down, and when he began to speak, his voice sounded funny, as if he were going to cry.

"Carol, you won't believe it, but late last night I sat alone in my office and was crying out to God with the bills in my hands. I sat there feeling surrounded by His presence. God felt so near, and it was as though I could hear Him say, '*Just trust Me. I will take care of you.*'"

While my parents hugged and kept talking, I climbed onto a chair and started pulling out boxes of cereal and cookies. It was totally normal for me to hear about God and the amazing things He could do. I had a front-row seat to watch genuine faith being lived out.

One morning, while Mom was vacuuming the living room carpet, I came and pulled on her sleeve.

"What is it, Chrissy?"

"Mommy, how can I get Jesus into my heart? I want Jesus in my heart."

Mom turned off the vacuum and sat on the old tweed chair. She looked me in the eyes and replied, "You just have to invite Him in."

"I want to *now*, Mommy."

She didn't hesitate, but took me by the hand and led me up the stairs to the guest room, where she knelt down at the side of the bed. I knelt down next to her, trying to reach the top of the mattress so I could rest my folded hands under my chin. She smiled and put her arm around me and said, "Repeat after me. 'Jesus, I believe that You are my Savior and that You died for my sins.'"

With my eyes closed tightly, I repeated every word. "Please come into my heart and stay."

My heart was beating a little faster when we got to the end of the prayer. "Amen." Amen! Mom explained to me what had just happened in words that made sense to me. Then she gave me a big hug.

That night while I was lying in my bed, my eyes scanned the framed prayer that hung on my wall. My great-grandmother had embroidered it and given it to my mom when I was born. Mom had read it to me so many times, I slowly whispered,

Now I lay me down to sleep,
I pray the Lord my soul to keep.
If I should die before I wake,
I pray the Lord my soul to take.

Up until now, the prayer was just something that I said every night and it always seemed to calm me for sleep. But tonight its meaning captured me because I knew my soul *was* His.

CHAPTER

3

ALMOST TWO YEARS HAD PASSED and things weren't really changing in our little church on Atlantic Avenue. We moved to Brooklyn to be closer to the people, thinking that might help, but the situations that came through the doors on any given day were getting more severe. From week to week, my parents had no idea what would happen next—like the time when my dad found out that an usher had "sticky fingers" while counting the offering in the ushers' room. My parents were gifted people, but gifting, goodness, and even sacrifice weren't making much of a difference. People trapped by drugs and alcohol came looking for help, but more often than not, they couldn't get free of what controlled them. I was oblivious to how discouraged my parents were since they never let the problems at the church affect our home life or me in any way.

My world felt safe and secure. It was perfect as far as I was concerned.

One summer morning, Dad brought me to work with him, and while he was busy in the office, I was busy too—playing in Rina's closet, trying on all her shoes. I loved the fact that she wore a size five and a half, because everything she had almost fit me. I put on a pair of white sandals with a T-strap that wrapped around the ankles and walked awkwardly into the living room. I edged my way to the couch, climbed up, and pulled back the sheer floral curtains so I could see what was going on outside. With hardly a cloud in the sky, the sun seemed overly bright, making everything look extra dirty and grimy.

I heard Dad's footsteps going down the hall and then down the stairs, so I slipped out of the shoes quickly and ran barefoot to see where he was going. I stayed out of his sight as I followed him. He disappeared into the church's small sanctuary and approached a man who was standing there alone. I recognized him as someone who had been helping out around the church for the past couple of weeks. When I had first noticed him in the building, I had asked my dad why the man was there.

"I'm trying to help him out, Chrissy, so maybe he'll get better."

That's what Daddy does, I thought at the time.

I decided Dad wouldn't mind if I came into the sanctuary right then. Skipping down the middle aisle, I jumped up onto the stage while he was talking to the man. I ran a finger along the side of the pulpit, then walked over to the organ, sat down, and pretended to be my mom. Reaching my small hand to one level of keys and pressing down on the lower level of keys, I wished my toes could could reach the pedals. The organ wasn't on, so I wasn't disrupting Dad's conversation at all. I enjoyed dancing my fingers silently on the instrument, hearing Mom's beautiful music playing in my head. Then another sound caught my attention.

Someone's crying.

It was the man next to Dad. Tiptoeing toward them, I saw tears running down his cheeks. I had never seen a grown-up person cry like that before. The man handed the broom he was holding to my dad and said he had to leave. I could tell by the look on his face that Dad was sad. The man didn't come back to the church again, one of the many people who wanted to get off the streets but couldn't.

Sometimes the things I saw made me afraid of "sin." If you asked me what it meant to *sin*, I would probably have said "It's doing things that make you sad." I saw a lot of unhappiness around me as a little girl, right outside the window of Dad's office. Our neighborhood was where a lot of sadness made its home. The man who slept on the cardboard mat outside of our church looked sad. The lady who got in and out of different cars looked sad. The man with red marks up and down his arms, whom Daddy was trying to help, looked sad.

Something started happening inside of Dad when he just got tired of the situations surrounding him. He began to get really desperate. Reading about times in church history when great things—even miracles—happened in particular places sparked a fire in his own heart. Every story he read had one thing in common—people got together and began to pray.

So Dad made a decision. It was a Sunday morning when he announced it to the congregation: "Before we depart on this beautiful day, I want to announce that starting this coming Tuesday night, we will be adding a new service to our weekly schedule. It will be the most important service of the week. We will gather to simply pray. Please greet one another as you leave today, and I look forward to seeing you all here this Tuesday night!"

It was a year later on a muggy summer weekday morning when Rina and I walked from the church to the subway station to catch the Q train. She practically had me in a headlock as we moved with the stream of people hurrying down the steps, trying to catch a train to Manhattan.

"Rina, where are we going? What's the surprise? Please tell me!" We watched a petite businesswoman yell at a man twice her size who was trying to push his way in front of her at the turnstile. She managed to squeeze through first and ran through the station, her briefcase swinging. It was the end of the morning rush hour, and most of the commuters were late for work, which was the perfect reason for some rude New Yorkers to be even more rude.

We made our way to the platform and I took a deep breath, catching the scent of ladies' sweet perfumes mixed with the mustiness of the run-down station.

"Today, leetal girl, I am going to buy you some Chinese slippers. I've been wanting to take you for some time now."

Rina knew that I had been dying to own a pair since the first day I saw them. They were the new fashion trend in New York City for women of all ages—a black fabric shoe with a thin, eraser-colored rubber sole and a small silver buckle on the side.

"Oh, thank you, Rina!" As I wrapped my arms around her, I noticed some young women walking by. One girl wore purple bell-bottom pants and the other was in jean shorts and knee-high socks. Both of their outfits were finished off with Chinese slippers!

They're so cool. Now I was beginning to panic. "Do you think they'll have them in my size, Rina?"

"Don't worry, sweetheart," she said, laughing. "They have every size and lots of them!"

When the Q train pulled to a stop in front of us and the doors opened, Rina did a little shoving herself to get us into the crammed subway car. There were no seats available, so Rina inched us to the closest pole so we'd have something to hang on to. It was ninety degrees outside and about one hundred and ten degrees inside. The only air that came in was when someone opened the door to go to the next car, letting a breeze through that would provide a bit of relief. A businessman in a three-piece suit stood above me, holding on to the same pole I was. I glanced up and watched as sweat started to roll down his face and fall to the floor like raindrops, missing my head by inches. Rina held me tightly with one hand clasped under my arm, facing her, and when the train lurched to a stop she half pulled, half scooped me off the train.

Canal Street! The steps that led to the street level beckoned me; it took everything in me to keep from running ahead of Rina.

As we emerged from the stairwell, it started to drizzle. The light rain felt refreshing after the steamy subway. Being in the car with Dad and driving through Chinatown was one thing, but walking through the crowded streets was another. The smell of fried food and raw fish, mixed with the overflowing containers of trash that lined the sidewalks, was overwhelming. The search for my pair of Chinese slippers had begun.

Rina stood close by while I grabbed every pair of shoes that looked remotely close to my size. "I think these will fit, Rina!" I squeezed my little feet in them, hoping she wouldn't notice that they were a size too small for me. "I love them! Let's get them!"

"Slow down, sweetheart. Let's get you the right size first," she said, rummaging through the tower of boxes. "Here, these should work." By now, the drizzle had turned into rain.

Rina haggled a bit on the price with the seller, paid what she had hoped for, and we started to quickly make our way back to the subway station.

We hadn't walked half a block when I asked, "Can I please put them on now, Rina? I can't wait!"

"Okay, okay, just a minute." She opened the bag and pulled out the cardboard box, helping me put on my new shoes. My first grown-up pair of shoes! I was so thrilled that I couldn't stop admiring them. Suddenly, the breeze turned into a strong wind, and the light rain became a downpour. We were running toward the entrance to the subway and trying to avoid the puddles . . . when my shoes became soaked. I looked down and gasped—my white socks were turning blue from the dye!

"Will my shoes be ruined, Rina?" I asked, nearly in tears.

"Don't worry. If they are, I will buy you a new pair. 'Cause you know I love you."

Yes, I do know.

In some ways, I guess I was the daughter Rina and her husband had never had, and she made the most of every moment we had together. Having them in my life was truly a gift to me, and I felt like I was a gift to them.

Around 7:30 later that Tuesday evening, while napping on the vinyl couch in my dad's office, I was awakened by noise coming from the sanctuary below me. For a minute, I was confused. *Did Daddy leave without me?* Then I realized that the sound was music and people singing. I went into the hallway and saw there wasn't a light underneath Rina's apartment door. It was time to investigate. As I hurried down the steps, the noise started to get louder. It was a prayer meeting night.

I walked into the sanctuary, which was barely lit. There were twenty people there, some kneeling at their seats and some standing with their hands raised toward the ceiling. I never understood why the lights were always dimmed for this service, except for the ones shining on the platform. But Dad wasn't standing there. He was sitting on the front row, and Mom was playing the organ off to the side.

Dad had his eyes closed and looked just like he did when I'd peek at him in his office. Even though he was leading the meeting, he wanted to blend into the congregation, too. I think he did this so that God would be in charge of the meeting.

Looking around at everyone's faces, I could tell that Mom's playing was touching their hearts. There was something about her music during prayer meeting that would make me aware, even as a seven-year-old girl, that God was in the room with us.

"Bless the Lord, oh my soul," Dad began to sing, and one by one the voices joined him, "Bless the Lord, oh my soul . . . and all that is within me bless His holy name." As the small group continued, it seemed as if the singing was bringing God closer and closer.

The sounds, the feeling, the comfort I felt was like being wrapped up in the warmest, softest blanket possible. I walked quietly from the back of the sanctuary down the middle aisle, and slipped into an empty seat next to one of my friends.

Dad told us to join hands with the person next to us and pray. Even though I had done this before, this time something happened. A warm sensation permeated my whole body, and I started to cry. As the sounds of the people praying filled the room, in that moment it was as if I were being hugged tightly yet gently at the same time; so loved that it brought tears of joy to my eyes.

When we finished praying, the woman next to me said, "Chrissy, did you feel that?"

"Yes, I did!"

For the rest of my life this presence of God—God coming so close that you feel like you are being embraced by perfect love—would both haunt me and compel me.

CHAPTER

4

MY DAD'S PASSION FOR PRAYER molded our church, but it was my mom's music that filled it. Mom would inevitably make a mark on our church with her incredible gift for music. It was just a matter of time. She decided to start a choir at the church, even though there was no hint whatsoever that there was any real potential. Little did we know that twenty-five years later, she and I would find ourselves on the way to the Grammy Awards. . . .

Our flight to LAX was two days away and Mom handed me a hundred-dollar bill. "Go to Macy's, Chris . . . they'll have something nice for you to wear."

I grabbed my car keys and headed out the door, then stopped. "Mom, shouldn't *you* be finding a dress for *yourself*? We leave on Friday!"

"I'll find something tomorrow, honey. Don't worry."

I drove down the hill and then made a right on Northern Boulevard, heading to the department store I had been to a hundred times before, all the time thinking, *I'll look, but I doubt I will find the right dress for a hundred dollars.*

Pulling into Macy's, I immediately headed to the dress department and pulled every formal gown in a size four off the rack. After trying on the first five dresses, I began laughing out loud in the fitting room. *How tacky can these dresses possibly be?* My chances of finding a last-minute dress were becoming more and more slim.

Then I pulled the last one over my head. It was floor length and sleeveless with a high halter-type neckline, beautifully embellished with just the right amount of silver beading. It was perfect. And the price was fifty dollars on clearance!

I changed quickly, grabbed the dress, and ran for the escalator as if I were afraid another shopper might wrestle me down to the ground for it. Halfway down, I was immediately lured by the shoe department. Browsing the sale racks, I found the most stunning pair of black strappy satin stilettos. I paid $34.99 for them and was on my way, with change to spare.

It was a beautiful early evening in Los Angeles, and we deliberately got out of our yellow cab away from the crowds. My mom and I giggled like two girls, knowing that we were probably the only invited guests who hadn't hired a limousine for a grand entrance. We walked around the Staples Center holding up the hems of our gowns so that we wouldn't catch and ruin them. After showing our gold-leaf invitations to security, we finally stepped onto the red carpet—my mom first and me following, giving us the perfect view for taking in all that was happening.

The glitz and glamour was almost overwhelming. Hundreds of lights were flashing, as fans and paparazzi were massed together, trying to glimpse the next star on the red carpet. As a reporter pulled Mom aside for an interview, I stood amazed at how far her pure and beautiful gift of music had taken her. Anyone who knew my mom would tell you that she was shy and unassuming, preferring to blend into a crowd, rather than be front and center. But after multiple invitations to the awards in past years, our family and the music staff had finally persuaded her to come tonight to accept the award in person on behalf of the choir, if indeed they did win. The choir's three previous awards had been announced with no one there to accept them. *Would she bring home a back-to-back Grammy tonight?* It was time for the answer.

Finally the nominees were being announced. "The nominees for best gospel choir of the year are . . ." The names of the other choirs barely registered in my head.

"And the Grammy goes to . . . the Brooklyn Tabernacle Choir!" My mom stood amidst the crowd of thousands, a picture of grace and beauty, as she walked down the aisle and onto the stage. I proudly stood and applauded.

Mom was handed the award and walked up to the microphone. "I thank all those who made this Grammy Award possible, but most of all, I thank my Lord Jesus. He is the only reason we sing. The Brooklyn Tabernacle Choir is made up of people with stories of how His power transformed their lives."

As she raised the gilded gramophone, she ended with, "I give Him all the glory today."

An hour later, Mom and I were seated in the second balcony, watching the rest of the televised program live. Madonna emerged from a glittering, silver limousine to sing and dance through her Grammy-nominated song, "Music." I was just waiting for Mom's cue. Halfway through the show, she whispered in my ear, "Want to leave?"

"Yep."

We ran down the steps of the Staples Center carefully, gathering up our long gowns and chuckling the whole way. I think we had more fun that night at our own personal after-party than we did at the event itself. We enjoyed delicious teriyaki chicken at a cozy Japanese restaurant. At one point, I noticed Mom with her head down, playing with her food.

"Chris, I don't belong at an event like that."

"Actually, Mom, you do. Even the world is recognizing the fact that your music is special," I told her honestly. A myriad of thoughts filled my mind. I couldn't get over the fact that Mom couldn't read music but had written so many incredible songs. I thought about those early days on Atlantic Avenue when she first presented to our little church the idea of starting a choir.

"If anyone is interested in being part of our church choir, come see me by the piano before you go," Mom announced following the service one Sunday morning. Only nine people responded, and she invited them to the first choir rehearsal that Friday night.

Several months later, I was sitting in the propped-open

doorway at the top of the steps leading to the backyard of the church. This was my favorite place to sit on Friday nights, with the breeze blowing by me into the sanctuary where Mom was working with the choir. The yard had been overtaken by weeds and was surrounded by a chain-link fence. Clotheslines that were strung across the block like Christmas lights connected the rusted fire escapes of the run-down apartment buildings.

As a seven-year-old, I loved this time of night at church, with the sounds of the city in one ear, and in the other, songs about hope and love. I heard Mom's voice. "Okay, altos, I'll sing the part, and then you just repeat it back to me. Sopranos and tenors, I'll get to you in a moment." Mom's gracious and encouraging attitude made untrained singers feel as though they could sing anything.

That particular night she taught them a song called "He Loves You." After sitting outside for a while, I came in and sat on the sidelines, watching Mom put it all together.

After about two hours, she had everyone stand. She began to wave her arms to direct them, trying to make the song actually come together. The choir began to sing and the sound they released was one of the most imperfect but beautiful sounds I had ever heard. Some choir members started to raise their hands in worship, and tears began flowing down other people's cheeks. As I looked at them, I thought about what Mom had told me the previous Friday on our way home. I had asked her if the people were sad when they were singing.

"Those aren't tears of sadness, Chrissy," she said, smiling. "Those are tears of joy because of what God is starting to do in their lives." There was something *holy* about the music and the words of the songs Mom taught that moved me very deeply. It was one of the reasons I went to choir practice every week with her. I wanted to be where that music was. But the other reason was because it was a lot of fun.

One moment the group would be serious, singing and reaching out to God, and in the next moment, they could be laughing hysterically and acting crazy. When Mom sensed the tenors were about to start goofing off, she would try to nip it in the bud. "Now choir, I need you to focus; we're almost done, I promise." If they were too far gone, she would jump right into the fray, acting silly too. She just couldn't help herself; just like at home, Mom loved opportunities to break out and have fun. Although she'd lose the rehearsal for five to ten minutes, it was well worth it, because the comic relief not only unburdened the choir members but also bound their hearts together. After facing a hard New York City week, the choir knew they had a place to call home.

The love that was born out of the choir released something special in our church. Even as a child, I could feel love calling people in from the streets. There was something about hearing people of different ethnicities—Puerto Rican, African American, West Indian—sing together that really showed what love "looked like." Despite the racial unrest at that time across the country, once we were inside the doors of the church, the walls that divided people seemed to crumble. We hadn't belonged to each other before, but now we belonged to each other because of love.

That love came to me not only from my Rina but also my Lorna too. Lorna was from Jamaica, and she was also one of my favorite people in the world. None of our relatives lived in New York City, except for my dad's parents. But because of my grandfather's drinking, I didn't spend much time at their home, so people like Rina and Lorna became my family, like aunts to me.

"Lorna! Lorna! Do you want to hear the song I can play on the piano? I can play chords now!" I said, jumping onto the stage when choir practice had ended.

"Of course I do, my darlin'," she said with her lilting Jamaican accent. Tugging insistently on her hand, I drew her to the upright piano. I focused intently on the keys and began to play chords on my right hand while playing single notes on my left.

"Oh my goodness . . . and my baby memorized this?"

"Yes!" I said excitedly. "I hear it in my head and then I play it."

With a big smile, she said, "You are reminding me more and more of your mommy every day."

Just then, Mom walked over to the piano, and Lorna said, "Carol, may I tell her?"

My eyes lit up. "Tell me what?"

Mom grinned and nodded.

"Chrissy, I have a special surprise for you."

"What is it?" I said, jumping up from the wooden piano bench. Lorna had planned with my mom the week before that I could spend the weekend with her, and Mom had secretly packed an overnight bag for my visit. I absolutely loved going to Lorna's! While we were driving to her house, I asked her again, "*Please* tell me what my surprise is!"

"Be patient, darlin'. You'll see when we get there."

What could the surprise be? Was it a toy? Shoes? Clothes?

We pulled up in front of her house, and when we got inside, Lorna asked me to close my eyes, leading me by the hand to her room.

When I opened my eyes, I gasped. There on the bedspread were two beautiful dresses, with matching shoes next to each one. The first dress had a high collar, puff sleeves, and layer upon layer of powder-blue ruffles. The next dress was just as pretty, a pale yellow chiffon with a light pink flower print. A wide sash tied in the back, with the bow's ends hanging to the middle of the dress. I ran my fingers over each dress, so happy that they were my own. "Oh Lorna! I love them! Thank you so much."

"I'm going to make you look extra special for Sunday. We're going to curl your hair with rollers and put on that pretty yellow dress." I could hardly wait!

Early Sunday morning we sat across from each other at the breakfast table eating saltfish and ackee with plantains. Lorna had big, bright-colored rollers in her hair, covered with a floral scarf tied around her head, keeping them in place. I felt like such a big girl with my own rollers and scarf tied around my head. There we were, a lovely dark-skinned woman with a little fair-skinned girl, laughing and enjoying a native Jamaican breakfast on a quiet Sunday morning. Another reason to love my world.

CHAPTER

5

"SUNDAY, MONDAY, HAPPY DAYS . . ."

Happy days. It was the theme song of my eight-year-old world. I had parents who loved each other, who loved me, and whose ministry filled my life with beautiful color, glorious sounds, boundless laughter, and happiness even in hard times. It also happened to be the theme song of my favorite television show.

Eating dinner as fast as I could, I hurried upstairs to take a bath and get my pajamas on. The nightly news was giving the weather report, which was my signal that I had fifteen minutes before the show started. I stepped out of the bathtub and looked down at my skinny, undeveloped body. I sometimes wondered if it ever would begin to change. Some of my friends were already wearing bras, and my body surely didn't look like my mom's.

I just knew I didn't like it when my baby sister walked in on me when I was changing clothes. I brushed the knots out of my hair and took a quick look in the mirror. My hair was getting longer, and it made me feel a little more grown up. *Oops, almost forgot my robe.* When I wore my pink robe over my pajamas, it made me feel just like my mom because that's what she did. Tying the sash around my waist, I made one more stop in Mom's bedroom. I grabbed a lipstick from her makeup drawer, slipped it in my pocket, and made a dash for the living room.

Hurry, hurry, I told myself. *This is going to be a great episode.* Each week, I looked forward to being with my "friends" on *Happy Days.* I scurried downstairs and got cozy in front of our big console television set. I preferred sitting on the green shag carpet instead of on the couch, because I could scoot up as close as possible to the TV.

As soon as I got comfortable, my baby sister came running into the room, with my baby brother toddling behind her. They always interrupted my TV time, a game that they seemed to thoroughly enjoy. When they were born, I decided that instead of being annoyed by their arrival into the world, I'd use them as a means to establish some authority.

"Now, Susie, you shouldn't be right in front of that TV; it's bad for your eyes. Come sit on my lap and watch with me. The show is gonna start soon, okay? So you need to be quiet now." Thankfully, Dad would come in and scoop the two of them up for bed, which always made being the oldest child glorious in my young mind. I said a distracted good-night, then got back to my spot as the opening theme song ended.

I watched as Richie Cunningham walked into the living room

of his beautiful home with his mom and dad sitting on the couch, when his sister, Joanie, came running down from her room. I felt we had a lot in common. Their house was neat and orderly like mine, and they had a great mom and dad like I did. Richie and Joanie would always have guy friends over, teenagers who wore sweaters with big letters on them and shiny penny loafers. There was one thing, though, that made their lives look quite a bit different from mine: They were teenagers. It seemed as if they almost always had crushes on guys and girls and went out on dates, or at least tried to. I wasn't sure what all that meant, but I figured that the more I watched the show, the more I'd understand.

The girls had on poodle skirts and cute tops, with scarves around their necks tied off to the side. They wore red lipstick, which I really liked. It seemed that they spent a lot of time at Arnold's, the neighborhood diner, meeting there whenever they wanted. The jukebox would play endless cool songs while Richie and his friends enjoyed milk shakes, burgers, and fries.

And then . . . the boys' bathroom door would open and out would come one of the stars of the show—Fonzie. With his slicked-back hair, white T-shirt, black leather jacket, light-washed jeans, and black motorcycle boots, he got everyone's attention right away. He would raise his hands and . . . *snap!* Every time he snapped his fingers, a different pretty girl would leave her group of friends, run over, and kiss him right on the mouth!

I knew exactly what he would say next—"Very nice"— before he turned away and walked over to Richie and the others in the booth. A moment later, another girl came through the diner's door, and Fonzie put his arm around her.

I leaned back where I was sitting to see if anyone was close by. *No one around. Good.* I reached into the pocket of my robe and took out my mom's lipstick. I removed the top, rolled it all the way up, and covered my lips with the ruby-red color. Then I put it away and continued watching the show, certain that my lips matched those of Fonzie's girlfriends.

Although my show was really funny, in moments like this my mind would wander off. Even though I couldn't see myself kissing Fonzie like the girls in the diner did, I felt secretly drawn to what the teenagers were doing. It kind of made me blush and feel a little embarrassed. I was really curious why Fonzie didn't have to try hard to get girls' attention like his friends did. He didn't have one girl, he had one on either side . . . all the time. It was as if he had some special power to make them appear and cling to him.

It was getting to the end of the night's show, so I stopped daydreaming. "Hey, Fonz," Richie said. "Where are you off to?"

I could tell that Richie really wanted to be like Fonzie, especially when it came to girls. Fonzie slid into the booth and put his arm around the girl with the red lipstick and said, "You. Me. Inspiration Point. Tonight. . . . Aaayy." The girl giggled and snuggled up to him. Ralph commented, "Well, I guess we know what he's doing tonight." To which Richie chimed in, "Yeah, there goes another conquest. I hear that Inspiration Point is . . . exhilarating." And they all started laughing and the audience started laughing too.

What's so funny? I didn't get it. Still, I always wondered what really happened at Inspiration Point. What *was* he going to do with that girl? Probably kiss but what else . . . ?

Just then, I heard the phone ring a few times in the kitchen. My mom was upstairs getting my brother and sister settled in bed and my dad was in the basement, pulling laundry out of the dryer. The wall phone had an extra-long cord so you could actually talk outside the kitchen.

"I got the phone, Carol!" Dad yelled as he ran up the stairs with his arms full of clean clothes.

"Hey, Lorna! How's our favorite nurse doing?" I heard Dad say. "How's it going in Philadelphia?" As much as I didn't want to cut short my show, as soon as I heard her name, I jumped up and ran to the kitchen. I had missed Lorna so much since she had left for nursing school.

When I came into the kitchen, Dad wasn't there. The pile of clothes was on the kitchen table and the phone cord was stretched into the stairway to the basement with the door shut. I knew I shouldn't, but I cupped my ear against the door, trying to hear what was going on.

"Lorna, you have to calm down. Lorna . . . slow down. Just tell me what happened. Lorna, listen. Calm down. Does he know? Please stop crying and tell me."

My mind started to fill with questions. *Did Lorna get hurt? Was she in a car accident? Why was Dad talking behind the door?*

"Lorna, does he know?" Dad repeated the question. Then there was a long pause. "Get some rest and call me tomorrow. Carol and I will be praying for you. We love you, Lorna."

Dad opened the door and came up the steps. He had a troubled look on his face.

"Daddy, what happened?" I followed him up the stairs toward our bedrooms.

"Lorna's not hurt, Chrissy, so don't worry." Then he told me that I should go to bed. Dad went into his bedroom and closed the door. I just stood there; my feet wouldn't move. I didn't mean to listen, but I heard my dad say, "Carol, Lorna is pregnant." I leaned against the wall, frozen by what I had just heard. I was confused, sad, and guilty all at the same time. Suddenly, more questions popped into my mind.

I knew how babies were made. Lorna would only do that if she were married. *How had it started? Maybe she liked kissing him. Maybe they went out to dinner, but what did they do then? Why would she do something like that?* I thought only mommies and daddies did that.

My parents told me the next morning that Lorna was going to have a baby. They said that when we make mistakes God always forgives us. If we ask Him to.

I had heard the word *temptation* many times at church. The Lord's Prayer says, "And lead us not into temptation." Now someone whom I looked at as a second mom, who went to church with us and really loved God, had caved in to temptation. I loved her, and it sort of made me feel embarrassed to know that she felt ashamed. What would I say when I saw her again? What would she say to me?

That night, for the first time, I had trouble sleeping.

And for some reason, something changed about the way I felt about *Happy Days* when I saw it. Every kiss made me more curious. Every mention of Inspiration Point made me want to know more.

CHAPTER

6

EVERYONE WAS BUZZING because it had been only a few months since we had moved into Brooklyn Tabernacle's new building on Flatbush Avenue. A year before, by a miracle, we'd found an old vacant movie theater. It needed a lot of work—it was pretty disgusting inside when we bought it—but now it was beautiful. The theater was completely different from the original church where my parents had started—the run-down little building on Atlantic Avenue. Now there were comfortable apricot-colored upholstered pews, carpet running down the aisles, and a huge chandelier hanging in the middle of the ceiling with smaller ones surrounding it. Everything was so bright and new, it made the Sunday service feel like a special event. It wasn't only the building that looked fancy; the people started to dress fancier too. Men in suits and ties, and women in attractive dresses.

The women in the congregation provided me with my own personal fashion show each Sunday because they seemed to pull out their nicest clothes for church. They took a lot of their fashion cues from one woman in particular—my mom. She was super stylish and had an effortless sense of fashion. Her look was always modest, but with an eye-catching edge. Since turning eleven I was starting to fall in love with nice clothing, and my love for shoes that had begun when I was a little girl was turning into a *longing* for them.

One Sunday morning, I entered the back of the auditorium, making my way down the aisle to take my seat near the front. Mom caught my eye as she glided across the stage to take her place at the piano. I always marveled at how beautiful she looked. She was wearing a candy-apple red dress that had black pin dots in the fabric. Her wide, shiny black patent-leather belt and her high-heeled patent-leather shoes with ankle straps gleamed under the bright lights.

I found my place in the third pew, where the choir members were seated. People continued to file into the room as the service began, with the musicians playing an up-tempo praise song. The congregation didn't need any direction at all—they began to sing loudly, clapping and swaying, a spontaneous rhythmic expression of their worship. The resounding praise coming from our beautiful rainbow of people was what I was used to—it comforted me.

Suddenly I noticed that my dad wasn't on the stage.

That's strange. He's always up front during worship.

One of the deacons came forward to pray for the offering before the ushers started passing the collection baskets. Just then, my dad walked up onto the stage. He looked a little worn out when he took the microphone to introduce the choir. The group, now numbering ninety people, filed onto the risers as Mom took her place in front of them. With the piano, bass, and drums behind her, she began to wave her arms, directing them in the first song:

> *In everything, give Him thanks, give Him thanks.*
> *In the good times, praise His name,*
> *in the bad times, do the same . . .*

As I looked around, it was apparent that the people all around me were just as moved as I was by the music. All over the auditorium people began to stand—one by one—until the whole audience was on their feet. I was standing, too, and looked up at my parents. Even though they were leading the meeting, they looked like they weren't conscious of anyone in the room except for the One they were worshiping. Dad's eyes were closed and I saw a tear running down his cheek, and Mom stopped directing and stood with her eyes closed and her hands raised.

The presence of God was stronger than I had ever felt before. Everyone's faces were turned up to heaven and their hands were stretched high, as they were pouring out their hearts to God. Wave upon wave of worship flowed from the congregation. The song ended but the praise didn't. The musicians kept playing, and it felt as though we couldn't stop even if we wanted to. My eyes started tearing up too.

Finally the sweet worship died down, and everyone began to

take their seats. Dad stepped forward to the pulpit. "Open your Bibles with me to the book of Romans, chapter 3."

I pulled my small burgundy Bible out of my purse. My grandma had bought it for me and written my name on the first page: "Dedicated to Chrissy on her 11th birthday." I had a couple of highlighters in my purse too and got them ready. When I found chapter 3, I smoothed the pages and looked up at Dad. He just didn't look like himself—almost as if he were distracted. While he was preaching his sermon, my mind started to wander—I was thinking a lot about my friends.

Lately, I had started hanging out with the teenagers at church between our morning and evening services. Hanging around girls my age just wasn't fun anymore—they seemed immature, and I realized I had less and less in common with them. They still liked to play games and run around, while I was starting to pay more attention to how I looked and what I was wearing. I didn't want to mess up my clothes and get sweaty; besides, I was way more interested in what teenagers talked about, how they would sit around having interesting conversations about things that were still mysteries to me.

I looked around to see if I could locate any of them in the congregation. *I wonder if they'll wait for me after the service today. I hope I can go to the pizza shop with them. Will they think what I'm wearing is cool?* I had so many questions running around in my mind. Like last Sunday, when I hung out all afternoon at the church with a group of them while we waited for the evening service.

Devon, Veronica, Janelle, Karl, Alex, Rosie, and I had been sitting in the middle of the sanctuary, scattered across three pews, talking about pretty much nothing. Alex and Rosie were the teenagers who were my closest friends. I would spend the night at their house and they would come to mine. Their mom was our volunteer youth director, so my parents really trusted her. Both Alex and Rosie were really nice to me, and I secretly thought Alex was kind of cute. I often imagined that the two of them were the reason that everyone else in their circle of friends was so nice to me.

Suddenly Karl said, "Hey, have any of you guys ever . . ." At first, it seemed like he was talking only to the boys. But then everyone became quiet and started listening. As Karl went on, I started to feel really uncomfortable. *What is Karl referring to? Am I the only one who doesn't know what that word means?* Some of the others were laughing. Obviously, they knew what Karl was referring to. Alex and Rosie seemed more aware than I was. I wasn't about to embarrass myself, so I pretended to know too. The rest of the afternoon, I kept thinking, *Should I ask my parents?* I decided against it, even though I knew the topic wasn't something that should have been brought up at all, let alone in church.

"Okay, I'm going to ask everybody to keep their seats and give me their undivided attention for the next moments." *This is strange*, I thought, looking up at my dad, still behind the pulpit. *Dad never says that at the end of a sermon.* I noticed the deacons sitting behind him, which was also out of the ordinary.

"There's something I need to announce today that is extremely difficult for me."

Difficult? What would be so difficult for Dad to announce? He definitely had my full attention, as well as everyone else's in the sanctuary.

"Last Sunday, we received a handwritten message from my associate." Dad paused. "He ran away with a woman in our church."

Wait a minute. My dad's associate? Dad has only one *associate—Samuel.* I was confused. *Samuel? He's married.* My brows scrunched up as I tried to think straight. I turned around, craning my neck, hoping to see . . . what? My brain didn't even know what it was telling my eyes to look for. Then it came to me. *Where is Samuel?*

Dad had stopped talking. His face was beet red. It looked like his words were all choked up in his throat.

As the news began to sink in, people all over the auditorium started to react. The man sitting next to me dropped his head and his shoulders began to shake uncontrollably as he started to weep.

A choir member was crying so hard that she seemed as though she could collapse. An old woman sitting a few pews behind me looked frozen, staring up at the ceiling as big fat tears rolled down her cheeks. It was as if time had stopped in that moment. The joy and praise music that had begun the service had been replaced with shock and devastation and the heartbreaking sounds of sadness.

Suddenly, it seemed as though my world were a mirror that had fallen to the ground, shattering into a million pieces. Nothing was clear. I couldn't make sense of any of it. What made it so *bad* was that Samuel chose to run away with my friends Alex and Rosie's mom. What made it *even worse* was who he left behind: my Rina.

I felt like my heart was being ripped apart. I couldn't understand how this had happened. I had spent so much time at Rina's house. From what I could see, she and her husband loved each other. *If they loved each other, what made my friends' mother better than my Rina? What made her worth doing that? Why wasn't my Rina good enough?*

The rest of the day was a blur to me. I didn't remember getting in the car after the service, the drive home that afternoon, eating dinner, or even putting on my pajamas that night. I just lay in bed, looking at the framed prayer on the wall. As I read it silently, I burst into tears.

How many times had I recited those words as a child? I just wanted to turn back time and be that little girl again, looking at that prayer in my old room in New Jersey. My mind was going to a place it had never gone before. I became aware of something I couldn't even name. I pressed my face into my tear-soaked pillow, drew my knees up into my chest, and tried to curl my body into the smallest ball I could, the covers wrapped tightly around me. I just wanted to feel happy and protected. I didn't feel safe anymore. Something died in me that day.

CHAPTER

7

"CHRISSY, YOU'RE SO PRETTY."

I stood in front of the bathroom mirror with my makeup sponge, scooped up a dollop of beige foundation, and smeared it across my left cheek, then my right cheek.

"Chrissy, you've grown so much, you look so much older. You're a knockout. So beautiful . . ."

Right on cue, my thoughts, that seemed almost like voices, started to taunt me. When I first heard them, I wondered where they were coming from. My head? The mirror? I wasn't sure. But I was certain of one thing—the voices always came and surrounded me when I was alone in the bathroom, getting ready. "So pretty . . . so pretty . . . so pretty."

Squinting, I got closer to the mirror and waited. "It's not enough, Chrissy. You need more," the whispers continued, and I answered the call.

There. Done. Perfect.

"Not good enough."

The strongest voice knew exactly what to say to hurt me. "More shadow on the eyes . . . more blush. You don't have the lips exactly right. Do it again."

I turned on the faucet, leaned over, and scrubbed my face clean. I had to start over. The mirror was right. I had to do it again. The mirror bullied me, and I couldn't defend myself. It kept saying the same thing: I had to be perfect.

I was about thirteen when it started. Throughout the day, my mind would be bombarded with the same question—over and over again. *Am I good enough to be chosen?* Whenever the taunting began, my insecurities would go off like an alarm, and I'd pull out a mirror or run to the bathroom just to check how I looked . . . to see for myself.

Like many girls my age, I was extremely interested in fashion; there was always a new magazine in my room. I studied them more than my schoolwork. Keeping up on the latest styles was fun, but the more time I spent looking at the girls on the pages, the more nervous I felt inside. Everything about them was flawless—their figures, their makeup, their clothes. I never saw any mistakes on their faces. Could I ever be *that* perfect?

I didn't want to be the "cute" or "nice" girl. It often made me think about one of my favorite movies when I was younger: *Grease.* My favorite character, Sandy, was a pretty, innocent girl who had fallen in love with a tough guy named Danny.

At the beginning of the movie, Sandy, the newcomer to school, wore cute barrettes in her hair, just a touch of makeup, and a buttoned-down sweater over a white round-collared blouse. I thought her outfit was stylish with its full pink skirt, bobby socks, and saddle shoes. But it didn't seem to get Danny's attention. She felt like she had to become exactly what Danny wanted so that he would choose her.

Sandy asked her friend Frenchy, who was part of the "in" crowd, to help her come up with a whole new look, leading Sandy to sing one of my favorite songs—and one that bad-girl Rizzo had originally sung to make fun of her: "Look at Me, I'm Sandra Dee."

I didn't fully get it when I was younger. But now I could totally see why Sandy felt she had to change. She wasn't sure that she was pretty enough just the way she was.

Sandy's makeover was dramatic. When she transformed herself—wearing skintight black leather pants, an off-the-shoulder black fitted top, stiletto heels, lots of makeup, and sexy "big hair"—Danny's eyes lit up. Sandy was fed up waiting for the kind of attention she wanted from Danny. She didn't want to be cute anymore; she wanted to be "hot."

Grease made me think about Rina, too. To me, she was perfect just the way she was. If she had changed, would her husband have stayed and not rejected her?

Despite what had happened, Rina seemed to be doing okay. I couldn't imagine how I would have felt if something like that had happened to me. Rina was a strong lady, though. After the heartbreaking news broke, she spent a short time with her family in California and then came back to Brooklyn. She was now a single woman abandoned by her husband, but she went back to serving in the church as she always had. It seemed like she cared more about people than the shame of being left alone.

Deep inside, I had a lot of respect for her. The problem was that I was changing and wasn't her little girl anymore. Besides, I had a lot on my mind.

Our church had grown to a few thousand people now and was becoming well known around the country. Because my dad was the pastor, I started getting even more attention, and that only made me feel as though I had to be more and more perfect. I had to maintain the image that I created in my mind—at all costs.

The service was packed as usual on Sunday morning, and I had a front-row seat in the balcony. The hustle and bustle of people being seated after the service began was distracting at times. I turned my head and scanned the balcony, checking all the way to the top row, looking to see if any of my friends were among the late arrivals. As the worship began, I automatically stood up and sang distractedly while I scanned the audience on the lower level. A woman with a beautiful tailored outfit caught my attention, and my mind wandered off to all the great dresses I'd seen when I went shopping. Dad started preaching, and I was miles away. I glanced down at my dress, excited because I had just bought it the day before. No one had seen my new outfit yet. I checked out my black sheer hose, making sure the seam down the back was straight. Everything complemented my black suede pumps that were gold trimmed with a lightning bolt design on both sides. The music of the closing song that Dad was leading woke me up from my daze. He began a prayer of dismissal.

This is my chance, I thought. I reached down and slipped my purse onto my lap. Leaning over, I covered my face with one hand as if I were praying. Slowly opening my purse with my other hand, I peeked in the mirror on the inside of the flap. Reaching for my lipstick, I looked to my right and left to see if anyone was watching me, and quickly applied a new layer. Before Dad said amen, I was done and ready to be put on display.

I headed for the stairs leading down from the balcony to the back of the sanctuary. I had taken only one step when I felt a hand grab me from behind. An older woman with a large white hat and a sequined sweater pulled me toward her. "Chrissy! Look at you, girl," she said in her rhythmic West Indian accent. "You so pretty, eh? And so big now. Do you remember me?"

She reached over to kiss me. *Please don't mess up my makeup.* I turned my head away from her lips and gave her an air kiss. *Mmmwah.*

"Yes, I remember you. Thank you," I said politely. Pulling my arm out of her tight grip, I rushed away from her, hoping she wouldn't follow. As I turned the corner at the bottom of the stairs, I ran into one of the teenage guys. "Hey, Chrissy. You look *really* nice today," he said as he looked me up and down. I felt myself blushing because he was seventeen, three years older than me. And yet, I was happy he noticed me.

I was almost at the lobby when I spotted Rina out of the corner of my eye. Her face brightened expectantly as she waited for me to stop and hug her close. But I didn't. I was on display and couldn't be the little girl she wanted. I rushed past her and caught the disappointment as it chased across her face.

I walked through the lobby, sensing that eyes were on me. It seemed like the girls my age, rather than just noticing, admired me. Boys were clearly paying attention but in a different way, I could just tell, especially now that I was making myself look older. For a moment, I felt less insecure. All the time, work, and pressure I had put myself through in the bathroom that morning faded away. I was becoming addicted to this feeling of being watched; being the center of attention was an emotional rush. My image was the most important thing to me now. I had to be perfect.

In my mind, the expectations were high, and I didn't want to disappoint anyone. Whenever Dad called me in to meet visiting pastors or singers, I had to be perfect. When my friends looked at me, I had to be perfect. I had to be ready—and perfect—in case I could sense the boys' eyes on me. And yet, that voice inside me continued to badger me with criticism, whispering "not good enough." As much as I tried to ignore it, I would find the nearest mirror—in a bathroom, on a car visor, or in my compact that I was often pulling out of my purse. I needed to check and make sure.

I didn't tell anyone I was struggling with wanting to "be good enough" or that what had happened to Lorna and Rina was still rocking my fourteen-year-old world. I just didn't want it to happen to me and was embarrassed that I thought about it as much as I did.

I needed some answers; I needed to make sense of it all. For a fleeting moment, I remembered sitting in that doorway at the old church on Atlantic Avenue, with the sweet sounds of the choir in one ear and the sounds of the city in the other. It was so much simpler then, but that was so long ago.

I felt like the answers were "out there"; it was scary but also inviting. I was convinced, right or wrong, that I needed to answer the question: *Am I good enough to be chosen?*

The morning sky was crystal clear when Dad and I boarded the 757 jet at JFK for an eleven-hour flight to Buenos Aires, Argentina. Dad had already made several trips to Argentina to encourage pastors and minister in different churches, but it was my first international flight. The flight attendants smiled at me, probably thinking how cute it was to see a father and daughter traveling overseas together. I chose a window seat and Dad sat next to me in an aisle seat.

"Would you like some blankets and pillows for your trip?" one attendant cheerfully offered.

"Yes, please," I said, and Dad took them as well.

Of course, I noticed everything about the flight attendant. She was really pretty, with reddish-blonde hair that was feathered back in the front. Her teal scarf almost matched her eyes, and her skin glowed.

Over the intercom, the captain announced our final destination, and the seat belt sign lit up. I made sure mine was properly buckled as the attendants took their places in the front, middle, and end of the aisle and went through the preflight safety demonstration with the oxygen mask.

When we reached cruising level, the attendant returned. "Coffee, sir?"

"Yes, please," Dad said. "Light cream, no sugar."

"And you, young lady?"

"Um, do you have hot chocolate?"

"I can make that happen," she replied.

Midway through the flight, we were served a good dinner. An hour later they dimmed the cabin lights as I hugged my pillow to my chest and took a deep breath. *It will be so fun having Dad all to myself for a week!* I leaned over and put my head on his shoulder. Dad looked over at me and smiled. "Remember when you were little and you would come to work with me sometimes?"

I met his gaze. "I do. I wish we could still do that." I paused. "You know what the problem is, Dad?"

"What?"

"High school. It's a *big* problem. I think I should quit and come to work with you every day."

Dad shook his head and chuckled. "Uh, yeah, nice try."

I settled my head back down on his shoulder, and he gently covered my hand with his. *Squeeze, squeeze, squeeze.* Our secret "I love you." I squeezed back, then drifted off to sleep.

A few hours later, I woke up and looked at my watch: 10 p.m. Dad was fast asleep. Pulling the shade up, I stared at my reflection in the dark window. This "mirror" was silent. I didn't care how I looked because I knew that Dad loved me no matter what. I slowly slipped my hand into Dad's, careful not to wake him. My heart melted and my shoulders relaxed as all the tension left me. I was safe with my daddy once again.

CHAPTER

8

IT HAD BEEN EIGHT YEARS since Lorna went through what started out as a painfully messy situation. Everything had turned around, though. She had returned to New York and was back at church, now a single mom raising a beautiful daughter. I wasn't as close to her as I used to be, and would often find myself missing those wonderful times we had shared. I was definitely preoccupied with other things, though I watched from a distance how Lorna kept continually getting closer to God. She and her daughter were a picture of what I had seen my whole life, and it was undeniable—the power of God reaching into people's lives and making them brand new. Actually, there was an explosion of miracle after miracle at the Brooklyn Tabernacle. I continually saw evidence of God's love and the way only He could transform a person.

My parents were as busy as ever, committed to what I knew was real purpose in life. They never stopped even if they were tired, pouring themselves out to us and leading us closer to God. The Brooklyn Tabernacle was like a hiding place and refuge in the crazy, chaotic city of New York, a haven where people could come and experience God again and again.

Naturally, you'd think I would have wanted some of that same power in my own life, especially with the way I felt bullied and harassed by my inner voice's demands. But I was in a fog. A fog that blinded me from seeing anything other than the need to be *perfect enough* or *beautiful enough*. Sure, power from God was fine for everyone else, but not for me, not right now. I believed that God answered prayer, and chances were, if I asked Him, He would help me. But for some reason, it felt better to handle this on my own, to keep it as my personal secret. I hadn't shared anything with anyone, let alone God. It was a private torment that I kept to myself.

Every day was stressful for me. The voice in the mirror never stopped bullying me. I hated it and yet I was also reliant on its counsel. And then a new voice began to sound in my ear. It was sweet and drew me in, becoming stronger than my tormentor. It spoke through the perfect channel, something that had been a part of me all my life. *Music.*

After I turned fifteen, Lorna decided to take a new active role in my life. She began inviting a group of us teenagers from church—guys and girls—to her house for the weekend. Maybe she sensed something about my behavior and was concerned, wanting to keep an eye on me and be available if I needed to talk. Her house felt sort of like a dorm, but with stricter rules. The boys and girls slept in different parts of the house. Maybe she thought it was safer to have us there under her roof than left to ourselves.

We always had a blast—acting silly, eating her delicious Jamaican food, but mostly listening to music. Typically, when we'd walk into the house there would be gospel music playing on the stereo, but after a few hours we'd switch it up and have our favorite albums on the turntable: Whitney Houston, Michael Jackson, and Luther Vandross.

I remember on one weekend, we all went to the mall on Saturday and I ended up driving with a girl who was a friend of a friend, someone I didn't know all that well. When we pulled into Lorna's driveway, we stayed in the car for a while talking. It was then that she said it.

"Chrissy, the reason why all these guys are hanging around you is because they want to be physical with you. They really want just *one thing*."

Everything in me went cold from my head to my toes. I was frozen in my seat, wondering, *How could she say something like this? Wait a minute. Is she talking about the guys who are my close friends?*

Her words were like a knife in my heart; could they be true? I saw her roll her eyes as if to say, "Duh, Chrissy. Why don't you get it?" Her expression plunged the knife even deeper.

It was early Monday morning and I lay in bed, curled up in my thick, oversized down comforter. The digital clock flashed

6 a.m.—too early to get up and too late to go back to sleep. I wrapped the comforter tighter around me, pretending it wasn't my most dreaded day of the week.

I turned over, covering my head as I rolled, hoping to muffle the words that played over and over in my mind. "These guys want to be physical with you." The girl's voice in my head was as clear as if she were sitting on the bed right next to me. Her words and my feelings twisted into a knot in my stomach. On one hand, what she said frightened me, and on the other hand, I felt even greater pressure. Pressure not just to put on a perfect face every day, not just to be flawlessly dressed, but to be *more than that*.

7:15. The clock radio went off, and to my delight my favorite song began to play—"You Give Good Love" by Whitney Houston. A temporary calm came over me as the words and instruments soothed me. Surrounded by music, I felt such a sense of comfort. When I heard a song, a warm feeling always came over me. My sweetest memories revolved around the gift of music in my life. Memories like driving with Dad through the Holland Tunnel and listening to the sound track created by the cars passing through; the treasured moments of sitting right next to Mom as she played beautiful songs on the piano.

Music had an unmistakable power that could move my heart, something that had been awakened in me not just through my mom, but through the congregation and the choir members who sang their life stories. I knew that what they were singing, they really meant with all their hearts; songs about who they used to be and who they could become. I embraced those messages with all of my heart, accepting them as truth, even though

I was too young to fully understand them. And why wouldn't I? The songs came true right before my very eyes—all the time. I distinctly remember the choir doing a song called "Tell Them," written as if Jesus were speaking:

Tell them for me, please, tell them for me
That I love them . . .

I grew up with the sense that music could move my heart to do whatever it said. I could just "tell" my friends and they would come to Jesus.

As I got older, music didn't just move my heart, it became my secret friend. It was the last thing I heard when I went to bed and the first thing I heard when I woke up every morning.

The fear of sin that I had grown up with had constantly warned me, "Don't do it," "Don't go there," and "Walk away." That voice was now being drowned out by new music that told me, "This is how you do it," "This is what you need to become," "This is what will make you good enough to be chosen."

It was time to get up or I would risk being late for school. *But I love this song.* I waited for Whitney to finish before I headed for the shower. As the water soaked my hair, the weekend comment pulsed in my mind. Toweling off quickly and grabbing an outfit from my dresser, I turned up the radio so I could hear it while I blow-dried my hair. Prince's popular song "Kiss" began to play.

I squirted a huge blob of mousse in my hands, saturated my tightly permed dirty blonde hair, and started sculpting. I picked up the hair dryer, turned it on medium heat, and leaned over. Prince's words rang in my ears. "I just need your body, baby . . . I want to be your fantasy . . ."

Holding the dryer steady with one hand, I reached up and began scrunching my hair with the other hand. I stared at the floor, wondering for a second about what I was going to do after school.

My eyes traveled from my ankles, to my calves, past my knees, then stopped. I wasn't a woman yet; and yet that's who Prince said ruled his world. My heart started beating faster as I thought about giving myself to a man. Suddenly I was afraid. I wanted so badly to be someone's fantasy, but I didn't want to actually do what it would take to be that fantasy.

I styled my bangs straight, then flipped them over to the side of my face. I had five minutes to be out the door. The voices and images crowding my head began to get louder. Was my body desirable enough to fulfill someone's fantasy? I didn't know the answer.

Picking up my backpack, I ran upstairs. I grabbed my jacket and scarf from the front closet and dashed out the door to school.

CHAPTER

9

I NOTICED THE TWO OF THEM IN THE SPRING. They were hard *not* to notice—tall, fit, good looking, and definitely causing a buzz among the girls. The two guys showed up together at church one Sunday. They appeared to be Latino, one about six foot three, athletic, with broad shoulders, and the other six foot one, with darker skin and fine features.

I was sixteen and wasn't fazed much by new guys who came to the church, since I was surrounded by the best-looking ones around. But these two strangers definitely caught my attention. As cute as they were, something else about them intrigued me. It was as though they came from "the world," an environment I was not really acquainted with, and stepped into our church, where they didn't quite know how to fit in.

For the next five or six weeks they came, never changing

their routine. They'd arrive at church, seem to listen intently, but then would quickly leave without socializing. My girlfriends and I concluded that they must be extremely shy. Still, I was distracted by them, and I was annoyed. These guys hadn't introduced themselves to me or even seemed to notice me like other guys did.

Why haven't I caught their attention yet? The question rattled me even though I was getting plenty of male attention. I tried to console myself with the fact that the two mystery men didn't really talk to anyone, but it still bothered me.

Finally, at a Tuesday night prayer meeting, I spotted one of them making his way to a seat above me in the balcony. My eyes followed him, watching where he ended up. Rumor had it that he was a baseball player. Someone told me that he was drafted to play professional baseball right out of high school. How exciting was that! He was wearing his team shirt and jacket, so he was pretty visible. *Must have come from a game.*

Tonight I've gotta meet at least one of these guys, I thought. The meeting was halfway over when I decided I would do it. *I'll conveniently run into him outside the church when the service is over.*

As soon as Dad said the final amen, I quickly dashed down from the balcony, hoping I could catch the baseball player before he left. I didn't see him anywhere in the lobby. My mad dash turned into a slow saunter when I stepped outside. He was leaning against a parking meter in front of the church, obviously waiting for someone. I froze for a second. *What was I going to say?* I was walking into uncharted territory since I *never* had to do the approaching. Feeling kind of stupid, I went for it anyway.

I took a deep breath and boldly walked straight toward him. "Hi, I'm Chrissy," I said cheerfully. I scrambled for something else to say. "Do you play baseball?" As soon as I said it, I wanted to take it back. *Ahhh, dumb question. This is not going well.*

"Hi, I'm Al," he said, smiling. He did seem shy but friendly. We talked for a few moments and then I courageously invited him to hang out with my group of friends.

"Hey, a bunch of us go to Junior's Restaurant every Sunday after church. You're welcome to come along."

He smiled again. "Thanks, that would be great," he said. We started to exchange numbers when his friend suddenly appeared.

"This is my friend Jaye."

"Hi," he said, shaking my hand.

"Hi, I'm Chrissy." I turned and continued to talk to Al, but I could feel Jaye looking at me. He had a distant, enigmatic way about him that made me slightly nervous.

"So hold on to my number and call me if you guys want to hang out."

"It was nice to meet you," Al said, and the two of them started to walk away. *Wait! I wanted to talk some more!* I was startled. I stood there feeling so *not* in charge of the moment, which was unusual for me. People typically followed my lead and did what I wanted to do, not calling the shots on their own. I didn't like this sense of powerlessness. I now had a mission: I was determined not only to get to know these guys but to convince them to be part of my entourage. I headed back into church, turning one more time to see if I could catch a glimpse of the tall, handsome strangers.

I couldn't get Al and Jaye off my mind all day in school, spending most of my time rehearsing what to say, what questions to ask, and working up enough nerve to actually call. I waited a day, then decided to call Al. I had never called a guy whom I didn't know or someone who wasn't clearly a "church guy." Would he be taken aback that the pastor's daughter was calling him? It wasn't my style to be so forward, but I had a compulsion to call.

I went to my bedroom, closed the door, and dialed the number. When Al answered the phone and we began talking, it was as if we had been friends for years and were catching up. He was so easy to talk to, and we instantly connected. He told me about his success on the baseball field. Ironically, Al had grown up just blocks from the Brooklyn Tabernacle and had passed it often, but he never set foot in the church until he was eighteen. He had experienced an incredible encounter with God on a baseball field that radically changed his life. If it weren't for an injury, he would have been on the fast track to becoming a pro. I could tell by the tone of his voice that he was still heartbroken over it, but at the same time he was excited to learn more about God.

Over the next couple of weeks, Al and I talked regularly, often for hours at a time. I really looked forward to his phone calls. We would hang out together often—taking walks in the city, going to restaurants—and I always had a great time. The first time we went out, he took me for Häagen-Dazs ice cream and a movie, but it was nothing like a date. There wasn't any romantic tension at all. It was more relaxed, like two friends getting to know each other. Walking out of the ice cream shop, I spilled most of my coffee ice cream on my white pants. We laughed it off, Al making me feel like my clumsiness was actually cute. Each time we were together, I found myself feeling less and less self-conscious.

Although we were forming a real friendship, I could tell that Al was going to get really involved in the church. That didn't interest me. I needed to explore something that was out in "the world." I wanted to find out more about Al's friend Jaye and began to slowly pump Al for information. When Al and I would make plans to go out, I began to gently encourage him to bring his friend along.

Up until now, the only thing I knew was that Al and Jaye came from the same neighborhood and were childhood friends who had drifted apart. They reconnected when Al came back home after his freshman year of college. He reached out to Jaye and told him about his new relationship with God. Jaye was up for trying out the church, since most of the guys in their rough neighborhood had become potheads.

The day finally came when Jaye joined a group of us after church. I was nervous, but I also felt comfortable because it was in my territory, with my friends. Jaye was very funny and had a confident air about him. Everyone instantly liked being around him, yet he managed not to divulge much about himself.

He had a way of looking at me that made me anxious and excited at the same time. It's like he held the look just long enough for me to notice, but no one else. He made me feel attractive without ever giving me a compliment. When he talked about music and fashion, it was with a real ease and authority that made me feel like his opinion was totally right.

I found out that he was artistic and was a photographer. I put the two together and decided that he had to be a very sensitive person. There was something very cool and sophisticated about him that allured me. I wasn't sure, but after just the first time I was with him, I couldn't help but feel like there was something between us. It seemed to take forever for us to exchange numbers, but when we finally did, I felt like he was totally in charge of how our relationship was going to develop—a first for me.

I nervously looked myself over in the mirror before I walked out the door. It was going to be my first time out alone with Jaye. It actually felt like I was going on my first date, except no one knew about it. I didn't have my parents' permission, and I didn't even tell any of my closest friends. Something told me that it was not a good idea to tell my parents about this guy—that they wouldn't approve and I wouldn't get my way.

When I was younger, I had always envisioned that my first date would be celebrated by people around me. I thought that a guy would come pick me up at the house and probably speak to my parents for a while before we left. I imagined looking back and seeing Mom and Dad standing at the door as their "little girl" went off on her first date; this wasn't anything like that.

As I had grown older, my conscience had hardened and wasn't as sensitive as it had been. I convinced myself that I wasn't being dishonest. It was just that I was a private person, becoming more independent, and had no reason to constantly share my business with anyone. My curiosity for what I was missing led me to become more and more secretive.

Still, I was torn because I knew that my parents didn't deserve to be treated that way. They had never been overbearing or overly protective. They really trusted me. But my private world was exactly that: private. I needed to find out on my own if I was good enough to be the one person someone would choose to be his alone.

The setting was right to find the answer. Jaye was a twenty-one-year-old man who had clearly seen and experienced much more of the world than I had. Even though I was a girl who was, in truth, naive and inexperienced, he had decided to spend time with me.

We arranged to meet in Manhattan in front of Macy's. As I came down the block, I spotted him immediately just by the way he was dressed. He had on a light blue linen button-down shirt with the sleeves slightly rolled up and light khaki pants; his camel-brown shoes and belt matched perfectly.

When Jaye got into the car, he suggested we head to Greenwich Village. After a difficult time of finding parking, we went to a very trendy Chinese restaurant that I had never heard of. The atmosphere was modern and sophisticated, and everyone there seemed to be stylish. Jaye fit right in, and I was excited to be welcomed into his world.

"What kind of music do you like, Chrissy?" he asked.

I responded confidently. "My favorites are R & B artists like Whitney Houston and Michael Jackson. How about you?"

"I like them . . . everybody does, but I'm more into Sting's music. Have you ever heard of him? He was with The Police and then went solo. You probably know the song he recorded with them—'Every Little Thing She Does Is Magic.'"

"No, I don't think I know it."

"That's just one of my favorites. I like his songs because they're deep and about real life. I think most music today is pretty predictable." Jaye began reciting the lyrics to Sting's song "King of Pain."

There's a little black spot on the sun today
That's my soul up there . . .

As Jaye went line by line through the song, delivering it with a poetic flair, I couldn't take my eyes off him. When he was finished, I was both mesmerized and intimidated. I loved music too, but I realized that Jaye wasn't just listening to the words; he was truly into music, examining a song on a deeper creative level than I was used to. I felt giddy but wanted to change the subject because I wanted to brush up on the music he liked before I embarrassed myself.

I quickly asked him, "Where do you work?"

"Well, I work in photo labs, but I do photography on the side."

"Really? What kind of photography do you do?"

"I've done different things. I really like fashion."

"You mean you've photographed models?"

"Yes, actually I've photographed some really beautiful women. That's just one type of project I've done in the past."

Suddenly, a wave of insecurity swept over me and I felt very small. "Um, I need to run to the restroom a minute."

He gave me a perplexed look because of the abrupt interruption. I got up, and although I wanted to run, I tried to walk to the ladies' room as if it weren't an emergency.

Walking down the dimly lit hallway, I pushed the dark oak door marked Women. Bright studio lights framing a wall of mirrors nearly blinded me as I walked into the room. Setting my purse on the dark granite counter, I looked in the mirror and tried to breathe.

I was overwhelmed by what Jaye had just said. "I've photographed some really beautiful women." Suddenly, his dark eyes transformed into a camera lens, a lens accustomed to perfection. He was an experienced photographer who was used to looking closely at models. What did he see when he looked at me? Was I even close to his standard of beauty?

I leaned closer to the mirror to examine my eyes, shifting my head to the left and right to get a better view of my face. All I could see was imperfection. I took out my "tools" and got to work, smoothing on more foundation and touching up the shadow over my eyes. I leaned closer to the mirror again, then slowly drew back.

How am I going to compete with all the beautiful women Jaye's captured on film and in his mind? When he's sitting across from me, so inexperienced and young, is he focusing on my imperfection and comparing me to their perfect beauty?

My thoughts tormented me as I stepped farther back to take in my entire outfit. Suddenly I was riddled with more fear and doubt. *Is this the right outfit? My body isn't perfect like theirs, but does this make me close to his vision of perfection?*

Just being with Jaye drew me deeper into this new world filled with sensuality. My naiveté frustrated me because I wanted to be alluring enough to capture and keep his attention. I knew I had been in the restroom too long. I had to return to the table, but now I was more weighed down and plagued by fears than when I had come in.

One more look and I will head back. I stepped back again, turned sideways, then faced the mirror again. I made myself a promise: *Whatever happens tonight, I am going to become whatever his lens considers to be perfect.*

Walking back to the table, the excitement I'd felt when we first arrived had disappeared. Now I felt like I was in an audition. As we talked, I began to cover my face with one hand so that he couldn't get a complete look at me.

Suddenly Jaye said, "Chrissy, that's a great outfit. I really love your taste in clothing. Every time I see you, you're wearing such stylish pieces, and you look really good in them."

A wave of relief swept over me. Even though he didn't compare me to a beautiful fashion model, his acknowledgment of my looks propped me up. That one line was enough to happily carry me through the rest of the evening.

Shortly after that, the shocker came! He casually mentioned that he had a two-year-old daughter. Not exactly what I wanted to hear on my first date—ever! My expression didn't change but I was reeling inside. Immediately, I thought about what my parents would think and who this woman was.

Does he still have feelings for her? Are they still connected? My thoughts began to race but Jaye's matter-of-fact tone made it seem that it wasn't a big deal at all to him. It was just another facet of who he was, but hearing those words made me feel like I was shrinking again. I decided to bury this information for now and deal with it later.

CHAPTER

10

THE RADIO HOST ON THE NEW WAVE STATION was giving the playlist for the next half hour. I was getting dressed the morning after my date with Jaye and was trying this station for the first time on his recommendation. My ears perked up when I heard the word *magic*.

That's it! That's the song he mentioned! I thought, almost as excited as if Jaye were going to come over for a visit. I dropped what I was doing and sat on the floor in front of my stereo, getting comfortable and entering into a total daze.

My thoughts drifted to the previous night . . . the great time I'd had with Jaye, and yet not so great either. It had been exciting but nerve-racking, adding even more pressure to what I had lived with for the last few years. Not only would I be potentially competing with a woman I'd never meet, who had his child, but even worse I would now have to compete with models he had worked with. Images from *Vogue, Mademoiselle, Elle, Seventeen*, and all my other fashion magazines assaulted my mind along with what Jaye had said at dinner.

For years, I had idolized the models in my magazines. Breathtakingly beautiful women whose perfection always tormented me. High cheekbones, wide and deep-set eyes, arched brows, amazing hair, without a single mark or imperfection. In every photograph, they were perfect, regardless of how much makeup they had on or what they wore. I bought the magazines because I loved fashion, but flipping through them always made me feel less and less beautiful, each image more tormenting than the last.

Needless to say, the bully was waiting to spew insults at me the moment I passed by the mirror. I didn't have the energy to deal with it. I woke from my daze when I heard Sting's voice. Closing my eyes as "Every Little Thing She Does Is Magic" played, I listened with every intention of embracing the song. Instantly I was transported into the music itself. The bass guitar combined with piano and strings had an unusual eclectic sound. As much as I knew about music, I couldn't peg it. The mystery of what I was hearing complemented the mystery of who Jaye was to me. It was as though *his spirit* was in the music. I wanted to hear more because it was so irresistibly captivating, so unlike the music I usually listened to . . . with an edge that pulled me in.

Every little thing she does is magic. . . . my love for her goes on.

The lyrics took center stage, telling me what was of utmost importance. Once again, my inner voice interrupted, advising me to ask myself if I was good enough to be that "magic" that would turn him on. *What does he think of when he listens to this song? What does he see? Could I be that magic to Jaye?* There was nothing I wanted more at that moment than to be that image. It would give me the greatest sense of gratification, the greatest fulfillment.

Even after the song ended, its melody and message followed me, clung to me. I began taking inventory of every part of myself, feeling more and more uncertain about who the girl was under the makeup and fancy clothes. I was so unsure whether or not I could be what I wanted more than anything. Even more than wanting to be the beautiful image in the magazine— I wanted to be *the girl* in the song.

Since Jaye had made only one comment about me and it was about how I dressed, I figured that appealing to his sense of fashion was my best chance of keeping his attention for now. I pulled my closet door open to assess the situation. Scanning from left to right, I looked over my wardrobe. It was quite incredible, thanks to my parents. It was really the only thing I ever asked for on a continual basis. My appearance had been my focus since I was thirteen. Hanging in my closet were high-collared pastel shirts hanging stiffly next to denim jackets and jewel-toned blazers. Perfectly pleated and creased pants with coordinating belts hung next to an array of beautiful dresses.

On the floor were my most prized possessions: my shoes. I bent down, admiring my favorite pair: pearly white tie-up boots with lace mesh-patterned cutouts on the inside and outside. I examined the two rows of shoes, neatly lined up. The back row, my boots: shiny black patent-leather boots with a diagonal side zipper, camel-colored knee-high leather boots with a cinched ankle, taupe slouchy boots that folded over, and black suede boots with zigzag patterns on the sides. The front line had pumps, brightly colored flats, and sandals. There were more than twenty pairs of shoes that I carefully arranged by color, shoe type, and season.

I stood there staring blankly, hanging on to the closet door. Although I had put tons of energy into this wardrobe, as I looked it over now, I felt so unsatisfied. I had an abundance of beautiful clothing and shoes, but they needed to be better. *I need some new clothes before I see him again*, I thought. My stomach fluttered like butterflies, imagining how he would think I looked. *I can't ask Dad or Mom for money again—they just bought me some really nice things last weekend. They'll think I'm crazy. . . . But I need to go to the store.*

I came upstairs to the kitchen, walking into a familiar scene. Mom was standing in front of the stove in her cozy robe and slippers, making us breakfast. "What can I make you, Chrissy? Would you like some cornmeal or pancakes?" she offered sweetly.

"Cornmeal, thanks," I replied distractedly. I walked over to the cupboard to grab a juice glass and looked out the window. Our home in Little Neck, Queens, was quite different from our previous home in Brooklyn. Living at the top of the hill gave us a great view of autumn's beauty. On days like this, I sometimes felt as though we were tucked away in an Old World European village hidden from the busyness of New York City, which was only at the bottom of the hill. The aromas of the season slipped in through the kitchen window: damp leaves on the ground, crushed pinecones, and the sweet smell of logs burning.

I could tell by looking at her that my mom was especially tired today. "How was choir practice last night, Mom?" I asked, pretending to be interested.

She gave me a weary smile. "Oh . . . what a night. We had ten people visiting from Norway who love our albums and came to the States especially to see how we do what we do. But Chris, it was a rough practice. Of all nights, the choir was not very focused. I don't know if it was because it was a long workweek or what, but they weren't really tuned in to me, or the song I was teaching them. I could do nothing to keep their attention. They kept forgetting their parts, and were chatty.

"Ugh! I thought to myself, *If there was any night I wish we didn't have visitors, it's tonight.* They just had to be thinking, *Does she even know what she's doing?* I had no other recourse but to stop everything. So I finally said, 'Choir, we are going to pray right now.' We all got quiet and began to wait before God. And Chris, all I can say is that it felt like His presence rushed into the room. The choir started to worship God and our practice turned upside down. It was incredible! As exhausted as I was when we dismissed, I thought that if our visitors only came to experience those last twenty minutes, it was worth their trip."

I began moving the cornmeal around the bowl with my spoon. "Wow, Mom. That's . . . that's great. So, what are you going to do today?" I asked.

She turned to me and her eyes lit up. "Nothing really. Why? Do you want to do something?"

I paused, sensing her desire to just simply be with me. To be close.

A part of me wanted nothing more than that—to spend the whole day with my mom—but I felt that my agenda was undoubtedly more important. "Sorry, Mom. I already have plans."

She quickly covered her disappointment, "Oh . . . okay. Well, I'm going upstairs to shower," she said cheerlessly. She set the dish towel down and slowly walked out of the room, perhaps hoping that I would change my mind. I sat there looking at my bowl, thinking about what was next.

Walking over to the sink, I put my dish in and waited. I stood there nervously, listening for the shower to go on. My heart began to race and a gloom came over me. Voices started clamoring in my head from all directions. Growing up, I had done a few "naughty" things but had never betrayed my parents in heart and spirit. Until now, my life had been squeaky clean, compared to even many of my church friends. I had never had a drink in my life, I had never smoked a cigarette, and had never held a guy's hand, let alone kissed a guy.

First of all, I knew my life was dedicated to God. I always had a sense that God's hand was on me. Second, the thing that kept me from sin was my *fear* of it—fear because of the consequences I watched it always produce. But now, suddenly, my mission to get Jaye to be attracted to me was dousing my fear of sin—really, for the first time in my life.

I found my mother's purse on the floor next to a chair and picked it up. I paused momentarily, as different Bible verses I'd stored away inside rose up in protest to what I was determined to do. *But I need to go to the store.* My mission took precedence once again.

I dropped the purse for a second and ran over to the window to make sure Dad wasn't home. There was no sign of his car. I grabbed the purse again, quickly rummaging through it to find my mom's wallet. I slipped out her credit card and then noticed some cash sticking out of the side. I took forty dollars and put the cash and the credit card into my back pocket. *Mom will never notice that anything is gone.* I called upstairs. "I'm going to take the white car, okay Mom? I just need to go get something quick."

"What, Chris? I can't hear you."

I was already out the door. Racing to the department store, I knew I had a short amount of time to get the credit card back without being discovered.

On the road, I began to draw images in my mind of how I should look and what I had to buy to make it happen. Visions of me walking into the room and Jaye telling me how amazing I looked started to make me smile inside. I drove a few miles to Macy's and began scouring the top name-brand sections of the store to find the best outfits. Piling a stack of clothing in the fitting room and soon adding a second stack, I began to try on outfit after outfit until I achieved the look I desired. I laid three supermodern ensembles on the counter, pulled out the credit card, and signed *Carol Cymbala*, replicating Mom's beautiful signature.

Thankfully, when I got home, Mom was in her room resting, which gave me a chance to sneak in my purchases. As I put the credit card back in her wallet, a sudden pang of guilt began to come over me, but as quickly as it came, I brushed it off. Overnight, I felt myself starting to ignore things that I had grown to accept as the truth, and somehow just dismiss every guilty feeling. It seemed like the tormenting voices and now Jaye were snuffing out the guilt, as if it were a candle being blown out.

CHAPTER

11

THE SKY WAS A SWIRL OF REDS, blues, and purples, with white wispy clouds creating a backdrop for the sea of cars on the Long Island Expressway. It was jam packed, which was typical for any highway leading into Manhattan on a late Saturday afternoon. As I followed the sign for the Midtown Tunnel, Manhattan's striking skyline was in full view. In my parents' white Mitsubishi, I inched closer to what had been my favorite place to hang out since I was old enough to take the subway by myself.

In the near distance to my left stood the Empire State Building—the image of regal elegance—and straight ahead, my favorite: the Chrysler Building. It was beautiful how the light of the sun caught the upper levels of the mirrored Chrysler Building, making it sparkle like a diamond. Farther away but close enough to still see, I saw the Twin Towers marking Lower Manhattan's skyline.

The traffic was crawling, so I pulled down the visor and added some more lipstick while I still had time. It was a shade called "Delicate Orchid" by Lancôme, matching the color of my midriff top, which hung slightly off the shoulder and was a soft knit with shimmery thin stripes across the front. My pants were baggy but in a flowy gray material with a high waistband, skimming my top and flattering my thin waistline.

Traffic came to a halt as I started approaching the incredibly long line for the tollbooths. I glanced in the rearview mirror and thought my hair could probably use a bit more reinforcement. Reaching into my purse, I pulled out the bottle of hair spray I always carried and began to pump short squirts on my carefully styled hair. Not realizing I had reached the tollbooth, I was thrown off guard when the attendant practically yelled at me, "Miss! You should really pay attention to whatchya doin'!" I jumped in my seat and dropped the bottle in my hand.

"You know, you can't be in a daze, hon, when you're driving in the city!" She waited with one hand on her hip and the other stretched out toward me for the change.

"I'm sorry, ma'am." My face flushed with embarrassment as I quickly grabbed the coins to hand her. Driving off, I was still preoccupied—I would be meeting Jaye in less than an hour. I knew it was a long shot, but I had decided to call him when I got home from Macy's, asking if he had plans for the rest of the day. When he told me he was free, I quickly laid out a potential plan.

"Why don't I meet you in the Village, on the corner of West Eighth and Broadway? We could hang out for a while and maybe have dinner together?" He agreed right away, and my heart started to beat a bit harder. This was going really well, almost too well.

I purposely didn't want to pick him up in the car this time. If I parked and met him somewhere outside, he would immediately see how I looked. I felt really good about what I was wearing and figured that I'd be able to tell right away what he thought. Making my way over to Broadway and then heading south, I repeatedly touched up my makeup at nearly every traffic light. To my left and right, the sidewalks were full of people, evidently enjoying their well-deserved weekend. By now the sun was beginning to set, casting a rosy hue on people's faces that made everyone seem like they were glowing. I cracked my window and breathed in the delicious aroma of roasted candied nuts being sold on almost every street corner, one of my favorite signs of fall in New York City.

I managed to find a great parking spot right on West Eighth Street, a few cars down from our meeting place. Stepping out of the car, I checked my pants for any wrinkles and admired my outfit again. As I walked up the block, a guy who was making a delivery said something very flirtatious to me. I purposely didn't acknowledge him, even though I probably should have felt disrespected or demeaned by what he said. I straightened my shoulders but I didn't feel angry. Instead I felt the opposite; his comment bolstered my confidence, confirming that I looked good and had a chance of getting Jaye's attention today.

I stood at the corner of Broadway and West Eighth in Greenwich Village, looking for Jaye to emerge from the nearby subway station. There was a slight breeze, almost enough to muss my hair, but I wasn't too worried since my hair spray was reliable. He was about ten minutes late now, making me a bit anxious whether or not he was going to show up.

I leaned my shoulder against the building, watching some punk rockers walk by with their super-high mohawks, dyed a shocking fluorescent green. I was looking in the opposite direction when Jaye suddenly tapped me on the shoulder, startling me.

"Hey," he said softly.

"Hi." Although I tried not to show it, I was upset by the fact that I didn't see him coming. I had hoped to read his expression as he walked toward me, positioning myself in such a way to be the display I thought he might like. But instead of feeling confident, beautiful, and in control, a wave of nerves washed over me. He smiled at me and said, "It's nice to see you."

"You too," I said, as I gave him a quick side hug.

Jaye didn't compliment me right away as I had hoped, but as we made small talk, I could feel him paying attention to me in a different way than the other night. His mannerisms said he was "into" me. I began to feel somewhat better about the way things were going.

We walked down West Eighth, peeking into the boutiques and shoe stores that lined the street. The more we walked, the more I felt a special connection taking place. While I was focusing on impressing him with my opinions about fashion, I sensed him focusing on me. Although he didn't say it, his vibe made me feel like this day was all about me. I started to relax. *We have so much in common.* Everything Jaye liked, I liked, and vice versa.

After walking for more than an hour, we stopped at Washington Square Park and sat on a bench to talk. We didn't face each other, though, because I was still too self-conscious.

He didn't push me to look at him; instead, he made me laugh. He made me laugh so hard that I couldn't help but come out of myself and be less guarded. Our eyes kept meeting and although I glanced away quickly, he didn't, and it made me swell with excitement such as I had never really known before. *I wish this day could last forever.* Every once in a while, though, I would get a pang of insecurity because I knew I was with a man, a man who was looking for *magic.*

We went to dinner, and this time was much better than the last time. We talked and laughed and he looked at me; it felt absolutely perfect. At the end of the meal, he pulled out his American Express card to pay, and while he looked over the bill, I found myself staring at him. *I can't believe I am on a date with Jaye. I love how good he makes me feel.*

When we started walking to the train station, Jaye said he had some things to take care of but didn't mention what they were. It just made for more mystery and more desperate curiosity on my part. I saw the subway entrance a block away, the wrought iron poles framing the staircase leading underground. I knew Jaye would soon disappear, and I wanted to make sure that the night ended right, but I didn't know what to do. I began to wish I could have gotten advice about what to do in this situation, but nobody knew about my rendezvous. My mind began to race: *How should I say good-bye to him?*

"Is everything okay?" Jaye asked, realizing that, all of a sudden, I wasn't talking. "What's wrong?"

"Nothing," I replied quickly. "I was just thinking about how I was getting home. Maybe I could go through Brooklyn on my way to Queens and drop you off?"

As soon as the question came out of my mouth, I felt stupid and blushed.

"Yeah, that would be great but I have to stop by and get some camera equipment from a friend. I'll look for you tomorrow at church, okay?"

I nodded as he looked me in the eyes and said, "I'll see you then." He leaned over and gently kissed me on the cheek, catching the corner of my mouth, and then he disappeared into the darkness of the stairwell.

A rush of emotions flooded me as I walked back to the car. I wanted to smile but I also wanted to cry. I longed for this man whom I really didn't know and became anxious, not knowing when we would be alone again. I had found *him*, and even though I was only sixteen, I just hoped that he would say the same—that he had finally found me. Driving up the brightly lit streets of Manhattan, I kept replaying our date as if I had videotaped every second and was rewinding it.

As I crossed into Queens, my thoughts shifted. *How am I going to convince Dad that Jaye is not only a great guy but great for me?* I began to compose a list of reasons why he was so special and so worthy. For one, Jaye was really gifted. My parents recognized the gifts in me and valued them, so surely they would have to see his incredible potential. Second, although Jaye wasn't necessarily searching for God as his friend Al was, the fact that he was coming to the Brooklyn Tabernacle proved that he was on a good track—didn't it? Three . . . I stopped.

Right now, none of those things really mattered. If Dad knew that I was out alone with a twenty-one-year-old man tonight, someone who kissed me good-night, it wouldn't be pretty.

Obviously, it was in my best interest to keep this relationship under wraps. *That won't be too difficult.* I was used to keeping things to myself.

The next morning everything was Sunday as usual. I arrived at church smartly dressed, thriving on the admiring looks I was receiving. But today, I wanted nothing more than to see Jaye. I saw him step out of the balcony stairwell and my heart quickened. Making my way through the crowd that was waiting for the next service to begin, I approached him, and he smiled when he saw me.

"Did the service just end?" I asked.

"Yes," he said as I turned around and followed him toward the exit. People were greeting me along the way, and I managed to greet them politely in return, while staying close to Jaye. "Do you want to go get something to eat?" I whispered in his ear. "We can go to Brooklyn Heights."

He looked confused for a second. "Sure. But didn't you just get here?" he whispered back. "Don't you have to go into the service?"

"Don't worry. Let's just go."

We made our way outside, in front of the building. "I can drive," I told Jaye, "but it would probably be better if I meet you around the corner and pick you up there. Is that okay?"

"Okay," he replied, not questioning me at all. I walked briskly back toward the church offices, wondering if my parents would notice my disappearing act. Moving past security and the secretaries, I reached my dad's office door, knocking twice, and then opening it. "Do you have a sec, Dad?"

"Sure, Chris." He had just finished preaching and was about to go back in for the second service. Dad looked up at me. "You look beautiful, Chris. I love that dress, too." Although my mind was on Jaye waiting around the corner, my heart skipped a beat. In moments like this, it was as if everything stopped and I was transported to the special times my dad and I had shared. He always made me feel like I was a treasure.

I quickly refocused on the reason I was there. "Dad, I was going to get lunch after the service and I need some money."

His smile began to turn into a slight look of concern, which was unusual. *Did he know something?* But I was relieved when he took his billfold out of his back pocket. "Sure," he said, putting some money on his desk.

His head remained down. "Who are you going with, Chris?"

I was momentarily alarmed; he had never asked me that before. "I'm going with some of my friends." Dad looked up and our eyes met. I could tell that he was trying to read me. I looked away.

"Is everything okay?" It was as if his eyes were piercing right through me. He reached out to hand me the cash. "Chris . . ."

Walking backwards toward the door, I grabbed the door-knob, "Yes, Dad?"

"Be careful, honey."

Jaye and I had lunch at a nice place in Brooklyn Heights near the promenade, but the entire time I was uneasy, thinking about my dad. Not because I lied to him about who I was with, but because of how he looked at me when he handed me the money. It was the first time he had looked at me that way—ever. It was as if his eyes were saying the last thing I wanted to hear—"What are you really doing, Chrissy?" I had done a good job keeping my cover, and my parents trusted me too much to have anyone spy on me. *What could he possibly know?*

We all got home from church pretty late that night. I was in my room getting ready for bed when I heard Dad calling me. I ran up the stairs and into the living room. Both of my parents were there, still in their church clothes, waiting for me. My blood rushed to my toes and I thought I was going to faint. Dad was sitting on the chair with his suit jacket on his lap and his tie undone. Mom was sitting on the couch with her feet on the coffee table, her high heels on the floor.

My dad's expression was serious. "Sit down. Mom and I want to talk to you." When he said "Sit down," the blood rushed back up to my head, flushing my face; the wheels in my mind started to spin. *Someone saw me with Jaye today and told them. I just know it.*

I slowly took a seat, anticipating the worst. *Dad's a very discerning man. I've seen him read people's hearts all the time. Or maybe God told him.*

Mom's eyebrows were knitted with concern as she looked at me. "Chris . . . are you okay?"

Pasting a smile on my face, I responded without hesitation. "What do you mean, Mom?"

She paused a second and said, "I mean, how are you doing?"

I tried to be nonchalant, reaching down and pulling up my socks. "Fine. Why?"

I could see her looking at Dad, giving him a cue to chime in. *The way she's looking at him . . . this is not good. They are on to me.*

Dad let out a long sigh and waited. "Your mom and I have

just been seeing a change in you, and we can't put our finger on it. It seems like you've distanced yourself, and we're concerned." *Whew! They don't know.* I acted surprised and disappointed. "But Dad, I'm in church every Sunday and every Tuesday! Shouldn't that be enough?"

"Look, Chrissy, your mom and I have always known God's hand is on your life. He's truly gifted you in music. And we believe He wants to use you in a special way."

Mom's voice cracked with emotion. "We're so proud of you, Chrissy."

Dad stood up, leaned on the chair, and looked at me, "I've heard great things about a Bible college in Louisiana, and we've been thinking that it might be a great place for you to go when you graduate. A place to develop your gifts and prepare for your future."

The tension I was trying to hide lifted off of my shoulders. *They are completely clueless. What a relief!* I was just so thankful they didn't know that I responded with the answer that made the most sense in the moment.

"Yes. I'll think about going to Bible college. I'd love to hear more about it." I walked over and gave them each a kiss and went downstairs to bed.

CHAPTER

12

THE CLOSE CALL WITH MY MOM AND DAD made me realize that I was slipping in terms of keeping up the appearance that their "little princess" was doing just fine. I decided to step up my efforts to make sure that no one in church would suspect that something was wrong.

"Dad, can I come in?" I peeked through his church office door.

"Yes, honey, come in!" Dad had that look of sweet excitement as I walked into a room filled with people. He came over and stood next to me. "Have you all met my daughter Chrissy?" he asked, as he gently touched the back of my hair. "Of course, you know Nicky, Chris."

"How is my beautiful girl?" Dad's good friend and special guest speaker, Nicky Cruz, embraced me as if I were his own child.

"Jim, the first time I came here to preach, Chrissy was probably . . . she couldn't have been more than six or seven!" I sensed Dad smiling behind me as Nicky held my hands in his.

I warmly replied, "Oh, it's good to see you. I'm graduating high school this year."

Nicky reached over to a few friends who were with him and told them in Spanish, *"Esta chica es igualita a su mamá. Le encanta la música, y se mueve y se ve justo como ella también. Lo verán cuando la conozcan a Carol."* Growing up around so many Latinos, I was able to make out enough to know that he was talking about me being like my mom as well as something about music.

I turned to his friends and smiled, making the flawless impression that I always did. "Dad, would you like me to walk your guests into the service and seat them?"

"That would be great, honey."

"Jim, is she coming with us to Junior's tonight? I want her to sit by me. She needs to tell me about her boyfriend."

Looking down, I responded shyly, "I don't have a boyfriend."

Dad joined in the lighthearted banter. "Hey, Nicky, watch it. Let's leave well enough alone, okay? Chrissy can get married when she's thirty-five as far as I'm concerned. Let's not rush things." Everyone laughed as we left Dad's office and made our way to the sanctuary.

I sat on the end of the pew with Dad's guests beside me. As a kid, I always loved the evening services. They were charged with so much energy, and without fail, Mom had the choir sing a few extra songs. But this night, I was more of a bystander, simply going through the motions. When it was time to worship, I sang with my eyes closed and my hands lifted high, while inside I was very anxious to leave. When it was time to greet one another, I shook hands and hugged the people surrounding me, while inside I felt pretty indifferent toward everyone.

Over the years, we had lots of guest speakers on Sunday nights, many who were well known, such as Nicky Cruz. Dad handed the mic to Nicky, and everyone cheered with great admiration. Inside, I wasn't interested in what he had to say. He began to preach, and although his English was broken, people were so locked-in to him that the sanctuary was absolutely silent.

At the end, he invited anyone who wanted to receive Christ as Savior to come forward. Within a few minutes, the altar was completely packed with people, streaming down from the main level, the balcony, and even the lobby where they had been listening to his message. I was done. I couldn't bear being in there anymore. I slipped out and went into Dad's office until the service was over. Afterwards I went out to eat with Dad, Mom, and the guests, putting on a pleasant façade to make my parents proud, while inside, I was very upset that I had to sacrifice a Sunday evening. It was the price I had to pay to keep everyone off of my trail.

Jaye and I were sneaking around often now. We were so good at it that our friends at church didn't even know. I was so driven to see him that lying to my parents had now become routine. I'd use both their car and their money, telling them that I was going out with friends when I was always going out with Jaye alone. Stealing from my parents to "attain the look" also became a

regular affair. Since I knew when Dad paid the bills, I methodi-
cally chose a different credit card than the last time to throw
him off. *He'll just have the impression that Mom used it for things
we all needed.*

As risky as it was for a senior in high school, I cut classes a
couple of times a week so that I could meet Jaye. My grades were
rapidly plummeting, and I was in jeopardy of not graduating
even if I went to summer school. I never let my parents catch
on, not even once. I'd tenaciously find ways to intercept any
communication from the school, carefully covering my tracks.

And my dad's dreams of me using my musical talents in
the ministry? That was the last thing on my mind these days. I
didn't touch the piano anymore. Actually I started to resent the
instrument, as though it were a person who was holding me to
a standard that I wasn't wanting to live up to right now. Nicky
Cruz may have thought I resembled my mom, and as much as
I would have liked to think I did, I didn't anymore. I resembled
less and less the woman she was. I'd watch her lead the choir
and I knew better than anyone in the pews that it wasn't just
her musical ability that made her great—it was her great love
for God. Although I still believed in God, I knew my heart was
far from Him.

Jaye was becoming, as Dad would say in his sermons, *an idol*
in my life. I was fully aware of that. The problem was, I needed
him. I was on a journey to discern whether or not I could be
good enough to be his one and only choice.

I started to detect greater concern welling up inside of my
parents. Even though they couldn't see anything wrong, their
parental alarm was sounding off. It was starting to worry me and

made my sneaking around more intense, which was wearing on me. They were not the type of people who would just accuse a person of doing something wrong, but they knew something was not right. I couldn't stand how it seemed like every time they looked at me, they were trying to read me. Sometimes, I'd even say, "What's the matter, Mom? Are you okay?" to try and throw them off by diversion.

It was 11 p.m. when we finally said good-bye to the guests at Junior's that night. They praised me to my parents for the way I hosted them. "Pastor, send this lovely girl to us anytime."

As we walked outside, I told my parents that I would see them at home and then drove off. I couldn't let the day go by without seeing Jaye, so I drove a few streets away from the restaurant and stopped at a phone booth to call him.

"I'm close by. Can you come downstairs for a little while so I can see you?"

"Of course."

"Okay, I'll be right over." As soon as I pulled up, Jaye got in the car. We drove up the block and parked in the shadows. We talked for a few minutes but immediately started kissing.

All of a sudden I thought, *This is so stupid—my dad has already been home for fifteen or twenty minutes now!* "I can't do this. I have to go."

"What are you going to say? You're definitely late now," Jaye said. "Don't tell him we were together or I'll probably never see you again." I told him to get out and walk back because I needed to get home as quickly as I could.

Speeding along the highway, I felt angry with Jaye for the very first time. It seemed like he really didn't care much about all of this and that he hadn't really looked out for me tonight. He wasn't the one who was going to have to face my father. He wasn't the one who had to tell the lies. He just helped me with suggestions on how we could sneak around and get together. Tonight, this whole thing was probably going to explode in my face.

I felt like my heart was going to jump out of my chest as I drove up the hill to our house. I knew Dad was going to be waiting for me. When I pulled into the driveway, I could see him looking out the living room window. He met me at the front door, looking concerned and angry. "Chrissy, where have you been?"

I looked at him calmly. "Dad, I've been driving around, thinking about my life, and um . . . I've decided that I'll go. . . . I've decided that I'll go to Bible school."

It was 3:42 a.m. when I finally sat up in bed after tossing and turning for more than four hours. I *never* had trouble sleeping, but tonight I had reason to. Over and over, my words replayed in my head. *I'll go. I'll go. I'll go.* My eyes darted around the bedroom in a state of panic. *What did I just commit to? Bible school?*

Reaching for my radio, I raised the volume to try to drown out the noise in my brain, but it didn't help. An internal debate ensued. *Chrissy, what about Jaye? Have you taken into consideration even once that you are leaving him? You'd be leaving the thing you want most right now. Then again, Daddy—how can you let him down . . . again? All he's ever wanted is for you to do well and be happy, hasn't he?*

Memories flooded my mind as I recalled how kind my dad

had been to me throughout my life. *Chrissy, what if he really knew what you were doing and what's making you happy right now? What if he knew how deceitful you're being?*

Now even worse thoughts began bombarding me. *What's going to happen if you leave Jaye? This is extremely risky. Jaye has every chance of starting a relationship with someone else if you leave. His daughter is only two years old, and he just left a relationship before you came into the picture. What would make him stay loyal to you? What glue is there to make this relationship stick, anyway?* I felt as though I were in a courtroom on trial and that the verdict was going to be awful either way.

I lay back down, digging my head into my pillow to muffle the accusations. I felt so helpless and confused. Lying there, I wondered for a minute how it would feel to live without this constant pressure that was bottled up inside me. I couldn't imagine what it would be like to just feel *free*. Free to enjoy being a teenager who didn't spend all of her energy looking in the mirror, lying and covering up her lies. I slammed off my radio, because even the music was annoying me now. Desperate for silence, I began to cry. I couldn't take the taunting any longer.

I stared into the darkness. All of a sudden, without invitation, a sweet presence came into my room. It was there, as real as the tears running down my face. I knew this presence from the time I was a little girl. It began to wash over me like a wave of what can only be described as love. I couldn't help but feel surprised that God would want to be anywhere near me right now. I heard His voice speak gently to my heart, "Chrissy, I still love you. I still want you. I still have a plan for your life."

As I cried in that dark room, I felt my heart become tender

in a way that it hadn't in a long time. My heart broke at the thought of God saying this, knowing my life had become nothing but a lie. Things were crystal clear at that moment. I was disgusted with the way I was now living, and knew that I had gotten used to listening to every other voice except that loving voice that visited me.

After a few hours of peaceful sleep, I was jolted awake by my alarm, feeling light and clearheaded. There was no doubt in my mind—it was settled. I was going to Bible college.

CHAPTER

13

AS SOON AS MY DECISION WAS MADE, the atmosphere at home became less stressful instantly. It was like an injection of joy and relief for Mom and Dad. Surely if I was willing to go to Bible school, things were now on an upward track. I could sense that the suspicion that had been nagging them for the last few months was now being replaced with some hope that I would be okay.

I was truly happy to see them happy. Making my parents proud had been something I majored on my whole life. Now I was making a great decision for my future, and that made me feel good. Maybe it was self-deception, but I even started to believe that all of this could make a way for Jaye and me to finally bring our relationship out into the light. I figured that if I were to get closer to God, then it was likely that Jaye would, too, and there wouldn't be any need to keep things a secret.

Maybe I'll inspire him, I thought. *Perhaps he could enroll in Bible school too*, I wished. The truth was, he needed to change anyway, to be the kind of guy I'd want to spend the rest of my life with. Ultimately, I would want a guy like my dad—someone I could trust. This Bible school idea was getting better and stronger by the minute. If God still had a plan for *my* life, why couldn't it include Jaye?

I called Jaye to tell him about my decision. He seemed genuinely bothered by the news. *Good, I want him to be bothered by the news.* It was my first real opportunity to measure how much he valued me. But as our conversation continued, Jaye's concern started to drift away, and he seemed to be indifferent to my leaving. "Chrissy, you need to do what you need to do. If that's what best for you, then definitely go."

I started to panic. There was definitely no *us* in his words. He seemed to be turning away from me in a single phone call. All the time together, all the sneaking around, even the affection we shared was being wiped away in one conversation because I was finally making one good choice. I felt like he was washing me off like residue on a dinner plate. How could it be so easy to let me go like that?

In an instant, I was crushed. Any joy I had experienced the last twenty-four hours was gone. My mind began to travel to familiar territory. *Maybe there are other girls he's thinking about . . . girls he will pursue with me so far away.* Over the next several weeks, Jaye's response to my leaving was just about all I could think about, but I really didn't say anything. I thought about that phone conversation just about every day, even when we were together, especially the fact that it really hurt me.

Graduation was just around the corner, and I started to feel miserable. The fear of losing Jaye was now mixed with feeling like I had disappointed my family. The big day arrived, and although I wore a cap and gown and got to throw my cap in the air with the rest of my class, I didn't receive my diploma that day. The whole celebration was spoiled by the fact that I would have to go to summer school to make up my failed classes. As often as I had cut classes to hang out with Jaye, it was inevitable that I wouldn't make it.

My parents were all smiles at the ceremony and didn't react the least bit, but rather made me feel special despite the big letdown. Once again thinking the best of me, they figured that public high school had been very challenging for me since I had been a "fish out of water." They knew I didn't curse, didn't smoke, and didn't have sex like most of my fellow students. They had never given me a hard time about my grades. And even though I would be spending my summer in school, my parents remained proud of me.

The following Sunday, Junior's was bustling with people piling in from churches around the city. It was always open late, and they had the best cheesecake in New York City, displayed in a case to entice you as you walked in from Flatbush Avenue. The atmosphere was always charged, no matter how late at night it was, and our table from Brooklyn Tabernacle would often be the loudest crowd. My dad and mom loved to laugh and loved to be with people. Regardless of how tired they were at the end of a long Sunday, they would host friends and visitors regularly.

Junior's was one of the backdrops of my life because I had

been there just about every Sunday night since I was a little girl. I would fall asleep many times right at the table, and Dad would carry me to the car and then to my room. The sound of laughter and table discussions about ministry and what God was doing in people's lives were some of the things that colored my world growing up.

This particular summer night, it was especially crowded, with people waiting in line at 11:00 p.m. for their orders. We were already seated and enjoying roast beef sandwiches, bagels and lox, hot fudge sundaes, and decadent strawberry cheesecake when I noticed a man from another table walk over and put something into Dad's hand. Dad got up from his table and walked over to me.

"Chrissy, come here a sec. Let's go outside. I want to show you something."

"What is it, Dad?" I said, totally confused. He didn't respond but starting walking toward the door, so I quickly followed.

As we were walking out of the restaurant, Dad passed the table where the man was sitting. Dad put his hand on the gentleman's back and said, "Thanks so much for everything."

We crossed to the other side of Flatbush Avenue and Dad handed me a set of keys. "How do you like it? It's yours."

There was only one car parked on the block—a shiny gray Mitsubishi Galant.

"What? Dad, you're kidding . . . right?"

The man from the restaurant had joined us by now. "I gotta be honest with you," he said, smiling at me. "It was really hard for me to sell this car to your dad. Not because I don't love him, but because I love this car! It has every bell and whistle you could possibly imagine—power everything, a sunroof, and control buttons all over the steering wheel. Let me show you all the features." All three of us got in.

I was stunned. *Could this be mine? My parents don't have a car this nice. It had to be expensive.* My dad's friend reminded me of a little kid showing off his favorite toy. I was sitting in the front passenger seat. I turned around, looked at my dad, and mouthed the words "Thank you!" When the demonstration was over, we got out and headed back into the restaurant. I gave Dad a kiss on the cheek, and before I could say anything he said, "You need a nice car. You're my Chrissy."

In the weeks that followed after the high of getting a new car, I went into a free fall of panic because my departure date for Bible college was drawing nearer. I was with Jaye incessantly, hanging on to every moment we had together, denying that I would soon be leaving him. The more time we spent together, the more I would make up stories, telling my parents that I was trying to see my friends as often as possible since I was going to miss them so much. What started out as one of the best decisions I had ever made had now become a smoke screen, drawing everyone away from how I was actually doing. The car was the last sign of how final my leaving home truly was—my parents' assurance of my finding God's plan for my life. But God's plan wasn't on my mind much now at all. Actually, I even found myself starting to belittle the way God had visited me that night as just something I must have made up. At this point nothing at all was worth losing Jaye for.

I was going through changes. We were spending so much time together, but instead of feeling the assurance from him that I was looking for, I left every date feeling more and more insecure about everything. He was still acting indifferent about my leaving, and it was like pouring fuel on a fire. My obsession to win his affection drove me to think about giving him more.

Our dates had been ending with kissing for the last month or so, and even then I felt guilty because of the sort of things that were going through my mind when we kissed. I was so naive, so inexperienced. Sure, I had desires like any seventeen-year-old, but I could feel my heart craving something more than any craving my seventeen-year-old body had. My greatest need when I was with Jaye was to know if I was good enough. I needed him to find me so special that he would never want to be away from me. One night I let go and did what I hoped might seal the deal. Jaye and I went all the way. We had sex.

It was 2:30 a.m. when I pulled into the driveway, and just looking at my house startled me. Everything it represented was everything I wasn't anymore. I turned the lock with my key and slowly opened the front door, hoping that it wouldn't creak on the hinge. I had never come home this late before; my parents probably thought I had been sleeping for the last three hours. I took off my heels and carried them as I tiptoed through the house to make my way downstairs. Every room was pitch black and the darkness accentuated how scared I felt. Yes, my heart had been growing colder lately, but not so cold that the little girl inside of me had completely disappeared. I felt more hypersensitive with every minute that passed since being with Jaye.

I walked into my bedroom and saw five outfits lying on my

bed; I had tried on every one that night before getting ready to go to meet Jaye. On my vanity, my makeup and hair products and jewelry were scattered in a big mess. Pulling my makeup bag out of my purse, I stopped and slammed it on top of the pile, scattering its contents all over.

I undressed to take a shower and felt more naked than I ever had before. I turned on the water, and stepping into the stall, I could see myself in the mirror through the glass door. As the water ran over my hair and down my face, my layers of black mascara began to bleed down my cheeks and onto my lips. I took the soap and a washcloth and started scrubbing. *I didn't want to do it this way! I feel so dirty!*

I toweled off and put my pajamas on, looking at the mess I needed to clean up. A tidal wave of emotions came upon me, and I didn't know what to do with them. I was alone and still felt naked even though my body was covered. Lying in bed, the numbers on the clock radio seemed to be screaming at me to turn on the music.

I didn't want to hear it. For just a few minutes, I didn't want to be the girl in the song.

CHAPTER

14

EVERYTHING CHANGED IN THE MORNING. I woke up needing to hear his voice, needing to know where he was, needing to know what he was doing at that very moment. I had given myself to Jaye, and now I was his. I didn't know that along with being intimate, I would also be giving him my heart. I didn't realize that they were attached, a package deal. As he was going about his morning as usual, Jaye probably didn't have a clue about what was going on inside of me.

I would usually call him from our home phone when no one was around or when I was absolutely sure that my parents wouldn't pick up the phone to make a call. Today I wanted to speak to him badly enough to take new risks, so without checking, I sat on the edge of my bed and dialed his number. Immediately my pulse quickened, and with each ring I got more excited to hear his voice. I could only imagine what he was going to say this morning, the passion that would be in his tone.

After several rings, he picked up. We talked for a few minutes about general stuff and my anticipation began to subside. It seemed like our conversation was business as usual, almost as if I were talking with someone I barely knew. Maybe I was just naive, but I thought it would somehow be really different today. That Jaye would be more loving and tender toward me. There was none of that. Actually it felt as though our conversation was more shallow than it had ever been.

I didn't know how to bring up my concern, so I asked, "Where do you want to meet later? I can pick you up."

"Wherever you want," he said.

"Okay. I'll pick you up at the train at six. Um . . . love you," I said, not sure I believed what I had just said. I waited for him to end the conversation.

"Chris!" I nearly jumped out of my skin at Dad's voice. I heard him running down the steps to my bedroom. "I've got to hang up." *Click.*

Whew. I didn't even know Dad was home. He could have easily picked up the phone. Oh no! Does he want to talk to me because he knows what I did last night?

The thought paralyzed me for a moment, as the horrific idea sunk in. Dad knocked on my door. *He knows! What will I say? What will he do?*

"Chris, can I come in?"

"Sure, come in, Dad." In the two seconds it took for him to open the door, I felt my life passing before my eyes.

"Hi." He smiled at me with the sweetest, most gentle expression. No doubt my face was two shades whiter.

"Hi, Dad." I leaned over and pretended to make my bed so I wouldn't have to look him in the eyes.

"Hey, I thought we could go to the department store today and buy you some things for college. Would you like that?"

I propped up the pillows on my bed, wanting to burst from sheer relief, but I smiled instead, holding my breath. "Uh, I would love that."

"Then get dressed! I'll be ready in fifteen minutes. How's that sound?"

"Great, Dad." I walked over to my closet, still averting my eyes. He started to leave the room but then came back in. "Oh, and I thought we could go to that place you love for lunch if you'd like."

My eyes began to tear up as I pulled a blouse out of my closet. "I would love that, Daddy." As soon as he closed the door behind him, I completely broke down.

I came upstairs, dressed not for my shopping trip with Dad, but for my dinner with Jaye. When Dad came into the kitchen, he said, "Wow, Chrissy, you look so pretty in that outfit! Hey, you think we could buy Mom something like that today?" Guilt assaulted me. *Dad always makes me feel like a princess, like the most perfect girl in the world.*

"Carol," he shouted upstairs. "I'm going with Chrissy; we'll be back soon." As we walked to the car, I realized that I was still shaking from the scare downstairs. Dad and I had not been alone like this in a long time, and today I carried a secret that would devastate him if he knew. The whole trip to Macy's, I did everything I could to act normal and not fall apart. His love and tender affection toward me was piercing my heart. After we arrived and parked, then Dad quickly jumped out, heading to the store entrance to open the door for me. "Chris, what do you think you want to wear at Bible college? Casual or dressy clothes?"

"You know, I haven't thought about that yet." I smiled at how thrilled he was to be with me.

Dad grabbed my hand and held it as we strolled through the store. He squeezed it three times and I glanced at him. *I love and admire you so much, Dad.* He was my security. When my hand was in his, I always knew I was safe. When I was with him, I never once doubted his love for me. Makeup or no makeup. Pretty clothes or just wearing my pajamas. I knew there was no changing his heart for me.

I could tell by the direction we were going that he was taking me to my favorite department. He knew from the time I was a little girl that one of the things that delighted me most was a beautiful pair of shoes. There they were, the summer's newest arrivals—bright sandals and heels in vibrant colors. The seats were all filled with women trying on stacks of shoes while others were analyzing their selections in the full-length mirrors throughout the department. There was usually nothing that could cheer me up quite like a pair of shoes, but today I wasn't interested.

"Do you like any of these?" Dad asked, picking up five different shoes. His expression was so hopeful.

"They're really nice, Dad."

He motioned to the salesperson. "Would you bring these out for my daughter in an 8½?"

I felt beads of sweat prickle on the back of my neck; my nerves were starting to fray. "Dad, please . . . you don't have to do that."

It was too late; there was no stopping him. The cashier rang up two pairs of shoes, and Dad smiled as he handed me the bag. Without saying anything, he took my arm and led me to the ladies' clothing section.

All of my favorite brands were there. "Chrissy, find some things to try on," he said. "Pick some outfits you really like." My heart ached because I knew that for my dad, giving a gift was one of his ways of showing me how much he loved me. It was coming from a deep place within him that was hopeful and pure.

Grabbing the first things I saw on the racks, I headed for the fitting room. "I'll be right out," I told him. When I looked back to see if he'd heard me, I saw him browsing the racks for Mom. I couldn't hold back the tears any longer. I pushed open the door to one of the fitting rooms, dropped the clothes on the floor, and collapsed next to them, sobbing bitterly. *How can I secretly hurt someone I love so much? What has he done to deserve this?*

Looking at myself in the fitting room mirror, I was disgusted not only by the clothes, but by the person staring back at me. I took some foundation out of my purse and smeared it under my swollen eyes, but the tears kept running. I grabbed a garment lying on the floor and wiped my face with it. I hated myself. If only there were a way to turn back the clock. *There's no way he can know that I've been crying in here*, I thought. *What reason could I give? If I tell him the truth, it will crush him. If I tell him a lie, it will crush him too.*

I came out of the fitting room with a few things that Dad quickly grabbed and took to the cashier. I didn't want any of them. I had a knot in my stomach and wanted to run away at that moment . . . if only I could. As I looked away, trying to hide my face from him, a couple walking down the aisle caught my attention. They were both good looking and were flirtatiously joking with each other. I studied them as they came closer. She was dressed provocatively with such an air of confidence about her. And the way he looked at her! He seemed absolutely crazy about her, evident in the way he touched her and how he gazed at her.

At that moment, thoughts began to ricochet through my mind. *This is what I want, what I live for. I wonder how Jaye and I appear when we walk down the street. Does he have that look in his eyes for me? Perhaps my clothing is too modest.* My mind had shifted so fast to these thoughts, I almost forgot I was with Dad. I looked down at what I was wearing. *It's all wrong. I need to be more like her. Especially because I'm going to see him tonight.*

"Chrissy, are you okay?" Dad asked, looking slightly concerned.

Oh no, maybe he can tell that I've been crying.

"I'm fine Dad. I was just thinking about the shoes you bought me, and how much Mom is going to love the things you're getting her."

"Okay. Are you sure?"

"I'm fine."

"Well, let's get lunch then," he said. As he placed another bag in my hand, I gave him a kiss on the cheek.

"Thank you so much, Dad. You shouldn't have done all this."

"Hey! Don't tell me what to do," he answered in his typical

fun-loving way. He grabbed my hand again as we left Macy's and walked to my favorite lunch spot.

At the table I tried my hardest not to show it, but I couldn't get the image of that couple out of my mind. *The way he looked at her. He was totally mesmerized.* I thought I knew what it was to feel insecure because I had been battling with it for so long now. But the imprint of that scene and the feeling the day after losing my virginity made me feel like I was becoming disconnected from everything and everyone I believed in. I could tell I was unraveling and starting to lose myself. I wasn't sure if I knew anymore how to be Chrissy.

CHAPTER

15

"MOM, YOU WON'T BELIEVE HOW NICE THESE DORMS ARE!" I paced back and forth, pulling on the long phone cord and admiring my new room. "I really love it here."

"Chris, that's wonderful! I am so thrilled that you like it!" I could sense her excitement through the phone. "How do the different things we bought look in your room? How's the comforter set? Does it fit?"

"Everything's perfect, Mom. And the campus . . . it's incredible! It's gotta be the nicest and best-run Christian school in the country, I think. Oh, and the students are just great! They're so friendly. Several of them have reached out to me and have really made me feel at home. When I introduced myself, they knew about you and Dad and the church. I guess there's no escaping, huh?"

We laughed together. "And they've commented on how 'New York' I dress and carry myself. One guy, with his strong southern accent, said, 'Girl, there ain't no way you come from anywhere near Baton Rouge, Louisiana!' I didn't know I had a sign hanging around my neck. It was pretty funny."

"Chris, are guys checking you out already?" Mom said teasingly. I could tell she wanted the full scoop.

"The ones who have introduced themselves to me, yeah, I guess, but they're not my type." Anytime my mom brought up the subject of guys, I couldn't help but get nervous that somehow the door might open about Jaye. In an attempt to change the topic I asked, "What's new with you? How's everything going there?"

"Everything's fine—just really busy as usual. You know, today I've actually been thinking that I might start a new album project. I'm leaning toward putting a few of those songs I played for you on it—what do you think?"

"Definitely. I think you should, Mom. There are probably plenty of churches waiting for your next release. Do it!"

Mom paused for a moment and then the cadence of her voice changed. "Chris, I really miss you." In that split second, her words carried me to the warm feeling of home.

My mom's presence was what had always made our house a home. It was going to be weird not hearing her voice every day, calling through the house. I would miss the way she laughed, the way she'd run back and forth to the piano while preparing dinner, filling every room with the most beautiful music.

"I miss you, too, Mom. It's going to be strange living so far away from home."

"Well, we can really look forward to Thanksgiving, then! I'm making your favorite meal."

"Yes! I can't wait. So how's Dad? Is he there?" I asked as I straightened the new textbooks on my shelf.

"No, he's still at the office with a few counseling appointments. Chris, I have to tell you. Dad took it really hard when you left. He's doing better now, but he didn't sleep very much the first few nights."

"Are you serious, Mom?"

"Yes, the first night I got up to see where he was, and I heard him downstairs. Chris, he was crying."

"He was crying? Why?"

"I was at the top of the stairs on the landing and heard him. It sounded like he was praying for you. He was crying out to God for you. I heard him say, 'Please be with her, Lord.' For us, you being gone . . . it's just something we've never experienced before."

My eyes began to tear up. I loved my parents so much. "Mom . . ." I paused. What I was about to say was long overdue. "I just want to thank you both for everything. I really think this is going to be a good place for me, and I appreciate all you've done—setting me up, buying me a car, and paying all of this tuition. I know I could've done better in high school, but I really want to make you proud now."

Without hesitation, she replied, "Chris, we've *always* been proud of you. You know that."

"Oh, Mom, I meant to tell you. They have a music department here at the school, and it has lots of pianos with practice rooms! I know I haven't been playing lately, but I want to start practicing again."

"Chrissy, I told you that you could be the best pianist in the world if you wanted to. You have a special gift."

"I know you've always said that, and I'm serious about getting back at it again. Well, I'd better hang up. I need to run down to the cafeteria before dinner ends. I'll try to call tomorrow so I can say hi to Dad. Love you, Mom."

"I love you, too, honey. Be careful." I hung up the phone and surveyed my dorm room once again, content with how organized and pretty it looked. *Wow, I can't believe how hungry I am.* I checked my watch—only a half hour left before the cafeteria line closed. *Hmm, I should get a sweater. I hate when the AC is blowing on me.* I put on my sweater, tucked my clutch under my arm, stepped into some pointy-toed flats, and headed for the door.

As I reached to grab the doorknob, I did a quick about-face. *My perfume.* I went over to the dresser and picked up the bottle, pointed it toward the bottom of my neck and squirted. As soon as the scent was released, I froze, unable to move. I took a deep breath. All of a sudden, a feeling as though somebody had died came over me. *God, please—I can't take this. Not now.*

A rush of tension hit me and my heart began to sting with each whiff of the fragrance. I broke down and wept, gripping the dresser for support. *I just hate this. I hate this!* My sadness turned into anger. *I've lost all control.* My heart was suffocating me, telling me that if I didn't see Jaye at that very moment, I couldn't make it. I thought about every possible place he could be tonight and couldn't shake the horrible thought of him with someone else. Jaye had me now. "I thought it would be okay. I thought everything was okay," I said through my bitter tears.

My appetite was gone. Dinner was no longer on my mind,

but calling Jaye was. If he didn't pick up the phone, I would be tormented by questions about everything. I tried to calm myself down, since we had talked a few days ago and things were just fine then. *Perhaps I'm having a premonition*, I thought. *Maybe . . . girl too far away + free time = find another one.* The possibility was gnawing at me, and I needed to find out.

I dialed his number, bracing myself for bad news. After the first ring, he picked up. "Hello?"

Thank goodness, he's there. "Hi. It's Chrissy."

"Hey! I was hoping it was you."

"Well, I was hoping it was going to be you! What are you up to tonight?"

"Nothing much. I don't really have anything to do and thought about taking a walk, but then decided to just stay home, hoping you would call me."

Wow. How could I even doubt him? My heart was overjoyed and so relieved. "How's it going there?" he asked.

"I miss you."

Jaye and I stayed on the phone for well over an hour. He told me about an incident at work that had me laughing so hard, I could barely breathe. His sense of humor made me fall for him all over again. We talked about all kinds of things, and I didn't want to hang up the phone even when we ran out of things to say.

As I got ready for bed, I couldn't stop smiling. Jaye loved me and my parents were as proud of me as ever; there was nothing more in the world that I wanted. I was actually looking forward to going to classes the next day. What was there not to like about this school? It was a totally perfect situation for me.

The next morning, the heavy, humid air that set Baton Rouge apart from New York greeted me as I exited through the dorm's glass door leading to the courtyard. *I can barely breathe.* I wasn't about to run to class, but my stride definitely picked up speed because I didn't want to be embarrassed walking in late to a classroom full of strangers. All the way to class, I noticed people glancing at me, taking in my clothing, heavy makeup, and the way I wore my hair. I suppose it was probably a bit much, me looking more like I was getting ready for a photo shoot than for an Introduction to the Old Testament class, but I liked the attention. I fed off of it, assuring myself that I was attractive and stood out from the rest of the students.

My first day of classes couldn't have gone better. Each class and professor was more interesting than the one before, and since I was totally dialed in, I started to feel like a real student for the first time in a long while.

By the fourth day, I became distracted. I loved the school and was making new friends, but with every chance to become more involved in campus life, to hang out and have a good time, I would start thinking of Jaye, and everything would be spoiled.

After the second week, my anxiety was becoming unbearable, and I knew I needed to see him. Talking to him on the phone wasn't enough; it was getting old. When I posed the idea of him making a quick trip to come see me, he agreed without hesitation. Two days later I picked Jaye up from the New Orleans airport. But from the moment he arrived, I was already dreading his departure. We made the eighty-mile trip back to campus, and the whole time, I debated in my mind what my friends were going to think about him being there. Classes were in full session, and it was definitely an odd time of year to have a visitor.

When we arrived on campus, I thought everyone was looking at us but figured it was just because I was especially dolled up with this handsome man by my side. I introduced Jaye to a few people, but I was extra careful to let them know that he was just a "friend" visiting me. I didn't want any word of this to get back to my parents. Things felt a little awkward that day on campus, and I told Jaye that it might be better for us to stay low-key and hang out elsewhere. I cut all my classes for the rest of the day and tried not to think about the work I'd have to somehow make up. After a day and a half of doing pretty much nothing, it was time for me to drive him back to the airport.

"Are you sure you have to leave?" Desperation started to well up inside of me, growing more intense by the minute. "Stay for just one more day . . . please?"

Fortunately, I didn't have to work too hard convincing him to stay another day . . . then another. When he finally left, I had cut four days of classes, and I had about as much interest in getting back to my studies as I did in joining the campus prayer team. A few weeks later I called Jaye and persuaded him to come back down to see me again.

The couple of friends that I had could probably tell something wasn't right, but they knew that there was this "private side" to me, and they didn't dare pry. By now I was holding my grades together with Scotch tape, and they were steadily declining. One day I happened to walk by a group of girls who were talking to each other, and when they saw me they immediately stopped, looked up, and stared at me in silence. I had made myself an outcast, facilitating gossip at this great school, but there was nothing I could do about it. When I wasn't with Jaye, I was extremely insecure and lost. Nobody was going to understand what I was going through, and the risk of talking to someone was just too great. Walking through the corridors on the rare occasion when I would go to class, I looked around me thinking how awesome the school was and how stupid I was for blowing this once-in-a-lifetime opportunity.

On a Wednesday morning in November I woke up in my room, realizing how late it was. *If I don't get to class today, it is going to be ugly.* The semester was going to end soon, revealing how poorly I had done. I lugged myself over to the window, lifted it up, and stuck my arm out. Louisiana humidity could be brutal—even in the autumn—and I wanted to see how bad it was. I pulled my arm in—it was wet and it wasn't even raining! "Oh, c'mon. Is this for real? Whose hairstyle can possibly hold up in this?" I mumbled to myself.

I quickly got ready, grabbed my stylish, lightly-used book bag, and headed to the elevator. My room was on the fifth floor, and I was getting off on the first floor. That was where the common area was located, a place between the girls' dorms and the boys' dorms where students could hang out together. The common area stayed open until our strictly enforced curfew at 11 p.m.

"You have a nice day too," I said waving to the two girls who were in some of my classes and had ridden down in the elevator with me. The student at the security desk said hi and gave me a warm smile as I passed by. It was crazy; despite the distance I put between myself and the students, there really didn't seem to be any pretense in them—they were genuinely kind. As I walked outside, I felt a slight breeze. *Maybe we'll finally get some real fall weather after all.*

My first class was in the farthest building from my dorm, and I hurried as fast as I could. I didn't want to be tardy because I knew I was going to create a spectacle just by showing up. Dropping my bag next to my seat, I sat in the back of the classroom and strained to focus on the lecture since I had been so disengaged for the last few months. Daydreaming was about all I could do for the fifty minutes, but I kept my eyes on the professor in an attempt to look engaged in what he was saying.

As I shuffled to my second class, I was pretty much in a stupor until I heard some guys talking about football and their plans for Thanksgiving. *Wow, I haven't even thought about Thanksgiving break yet. I'm sure Dad's going to call me any day now to try to arrange my flight. When is it, anyway?* I reached in my purse and pulled out a folded up piece of paper with the school calendar printed on it. I stretched it out and looked for the shaded dates. *Great. It starts a week from Monday. I think I'll get a flight for next Friday after my last class and . . .*

Suddenly, halfway through my thought, another idea popped into my head, an idea that made perfect sense. *Maybe it would be better if I didn't go home for Thanksgiving. Chances are, if I go home I won't get much time to be with Jaye. And even worse, I'll have the stress of making up stories to go see him anyway. He should come down here again, but this time for a whole week. I'm gonna call him. I know he'll come.*

The rest of the day was a real drag, and I spent most of my time thinking of an excuse I could give my parents for wanting to stay on campus for the holiday. My first thought was to say that I wanted to save them some money since Christmas would be a few weeks later. But knowing my Dad, he would probably insist and tell me not to worry about the expense.

Then I remembered hearing some students talking over lunch about not being able to go home for the holidays because money was tight.

That's it, I thought. *I'll just tell them that my heart really goes out to the students who can't go home and that I think I should stay here with them. They'd only respect me for that.*

I called home that evening and gave Dad my pseudo heartfelt story about how I could really be a blessing on campus over Thanksgiving. He completely bought it, saying that they would really miss me.

"And Dad . . . one more thing. Since I'm going to be staying down here, I was wondering if you could send me some extra money."

"Sure, honey, how much do you need?"

"Well, whatever you can send will be fine, but I thought I could maybe treat some students to a meal or two at a restaurant."

"I'll put a check in the mail tomorrow." He paused, then said, "Wow, I know this change in plans is really going to disappoint your mom, but if you really feel you want to do this . . ."

"Yeah, Dad, I think it's a good thing."

"Well, all right. I love you. Call me soon, okay?"

"I will, Dad. Love you too."

I didn't even set the receiver down; I pushed the button to get a new dial tone. The phone rang a few times and Jaye's sister answered. "Hello?"

"Hi, this is Chrissy. Is Jaye home?"

"Yeah, he's home, but could you not call here so much? Every time I'm expecting a call, it's always you calling. You're tying up our phone!"

I heard Jaye's voice in the background, then he was on the line. "Chrissy, hold on," he said. Jaye must have covered the receiver because I could hear some muffled arguing.

"Hi, I'm sorry about that," he said. "How are you?"

I hid that I was hurt by his sister's words. "I'm doing okay. I won't keep you long. I just wanted to see if you would come down here for Thanksgiving? We could be together for a whole week!"

"Oh, Chris, unfortunately I can't. I'd risk losing my job, and I don't have any money."

I quickly cut in. "Don't worry about the money—I'll have some in a few days. I'm sure it'll be enough for your ticket." Not giving him a second to interject, I said, "And just tell your boss that you have a family emergency."

After a few short minutes of persuasion—doing what I did best—Jaye agreed and it was settled. It would be my first Thanksgiving with Jaye and the first away from my family.

CHAPTER

16

I PULLED UP OUTSIDE OF ARRIVALS at the New Orleans airport and scanned the crowd of passengers awaiting curbside pickups. Jaye didn't see me, but I saw him immediately. His model-like physique was dressed in the colors of autumn—a soft olive-green shirt complemented by a coffee-colored leather jacket. I was really flattered. *People must think he's meeting someone very special.* The joy I felt at that moment energized me and made me feel alive again.

In a flash I forgot about the last few weeks of school; the sleepy monotony of it all was shaken off like water off a dog. Just the sight of Jaye made everything better. As he threw his bags in the backseat, I jumped out of the car and ran around to greet him. "I missed you even more this time," I softly said, as we shared a sweet kiss and tight embrace.

I couldn't believe this was happening. I had Jaye all to myself—not for just a few days, but for my entire Thanksgiving break. "It's such a beautiful day! Let's open the sunroof." We drove off and I began to activate all the great features of my car. "Oh, and wait till you see what's in my glove compartment! I bought it for us to listen to this week. Grab the cassette in there," I said excitedly.

He recognized it immediately. "No way! *You* bought *The Dream of the Blue Turtles?* I knew I would convert you before long." He pushed it into the cassette deck and turned up the volume.

"I really do love the whole album," I said, "but found it pretty crazy that my favorite song is 'Moon over Bourbon Street.' I mean, you *do* know where we are going today, right?"

"Let me guess," he said. "To the most famous street in this city?" He laughed, and I was thrilled that I had impressed him with my new affection for Sting's music. Following the highway signs to New Orleans, I reached over and turned up the volume a bit more. As the car picked up speed, the wind started blowing through the sunroof a little too strong for my hairdo. I guess Jaye caught me trying to fix it in the rearview mirror and eased my mind. "Don't worry, it looks great. Actually, you look fantastic today." I was always elated when he complimented me.

When we finally arrived, Jaye and I strolled around the French Quarter. Being out in public with a good-looking guy like him gave me a sense of maturity and sophistication that put a sashay in my walk. I hung on to his arm as we ventured down cobblestone sidewalks, peeking into interesting art galleries and antique shops. The area was a great fit for him because he had such an incredible eye for artistic things.

I loved that he held my hand as we shared a messy but

delicious beignet from Café Du Monde, spilling powdered sugar all over ourselves. I was comfortable with him; it felt almost as if we were already married, with everyone thinking that we belonged to each other. After a few hours we sat at the waterfront watching the ferry go by, and I leaned on his shoulder in quiet bliss. When the sun began to set, I broke the silence. "Are you hungry? I'm ready for dinner if you are."

"I'm ready."

"Well, there's an adorable café I noticed right off of Bourbon Street. What do you think?"

"Sounds great," he said, sneaking a kiss.

The setting sun was the perfect backdrop for the things that made New Orleans so romantic—horse-drawn carriages, street musicians, and sidewalk artists under streetlamps wherever we looked.

As we walked into the café the hostess asked us if we wanted to dine alfresco, and we answered yes in unison. She laughed, escorting us to an intimate corner. We took our time savoring every bite of our Cajun comfort food and relaxed while watching the sun go down. As Jaye commented about the great food, I began to silently count the days that he would be with me. If today was any indication, it was a start to what I imagined would be an incredible week—some quality time and a great chance to get closer as a couple.

The climate of the French Quarter began to "heat up" as we were ordering dessert. The jazz music that spilled out of the bars lining the street seemed to be dialed up a few notches; people were dancing pretty much wherever they wanted. The quick change in the atmosphere made me nervous.

"This place is feeling a little creepy, don't you think? It's like all of a sudden the vibe shifted," I said.

Jaye seemed oblivious as he took another bite of his bread pudding. "I did notice the music has gotten louder, that's about it. This *is* a big party town, you know. People come from all over . . ."

For an instant I tuned him out. *How can I still be sensitive to spiritual things when my heart is so cold toward God?* Ever since I was a little girl, I had been exposed to not just *light* but *darkness*, too. There was clearly something very dark in the air, and it was making me uneasy as Jaye was talking.

"Could you ever live here?" I asked him, always wishing the subject of our future might come up.

"It's okay, but I don't think so. I'm used to New York."

I reacted without really thinking, an independent spirit surfacing. "Well, as for *me*, I feel like I can live pretty much anywhere. I have to say the people I've met here at school are really nice."

"That, I *wouldn't know*," he responded abruptly.

"You wouldn't know what?"

"What the students are like."

"But I introduced you to some students the first time you visited me. What did you think of them?"

"Oh, you mean those guys? Those guys who obviously *liked* you? They were fake, in my opinion, and you never even introduced me to them as your boyfriend."

"Jaye, how could I? Things would get back to my parents."

"*And?*"

"And? How can you even ask me that? Are you forgetting

what I've been through . . . all the stories I've conjured up, all the lies I've told?"

"Well, just tell them, then. I'm tired of this."

"Tell them? Why don't *you* tell them? Then again, you've never even had a conversation with my dad! And you sure didn't have a problem with me lying to them."

"You should quiet down," he said. "Maybe this wasn't a good idea, me coming down here. You should have gone home to be with your parents." His words were paralyzing. I didn't want him to leave.

"No, no, no! I'm so sorry. I didn't mean to get upset. We are going to have such a great week! Forget I even said it . . . please!"

The ride to his hotel was very tense, even though I did everything I could to lighten things.

"Hey, I have a great idea for breakfast tomorrow!" I looked over at him, and his body language was clearly letting me know that he really didn't want to talk. I churned inside, fighting what was going on in my mind. The fact that he was upset made me so angry. I had given him everything, and he was disappointed in *me*? But my desperate need to keep him happy so that he wouldn't leave me ruled the moment. "Jaye, really. I'm so sorry. You've taken time off to come here and be with me. Today was such a great day, and I let it end in an argument. That was so stupid of me."

"Well, I'm thinking about leaving tomorrow, so just call me in the morning," he said as he opened the door to get out.

"No, really, Jaye. Let's just forget about this, please?" My voice began to crack. He grabbed his suitcase from the backseat without saying a word. I lowered the window. "Jaye, please don't leave like this . . . please forgive me."

He paused a second, put his bag down, and leaned on the door, sticking his head in the window. "Chris, get a good night's rest and I'll see you in the morning, okay?"

"Okay." He looked me in the eyes and then walked away.

Slowly driving off, I pushed the button to close the window and grabbed the steering wheel tightly. A surge of tears streamed down my face, so strong that I couldn't see the road.

Weariness seeped into my bones and left me feeling drained and hopeless. "Don't leave!" My voice echoed, frustrated and hopeless in the empty car. "You can't leave. I've done this for you!" I couldn't catch my breath, all at once consumed by everything I had done. Losing my virginity over the summer, psyching myself up to move away from home, sensing the students distancing themselves from me, hiding Jaye every time he came to visit, and most of all, living with the endless anxiety of being "less" than what Jaye really wanted.

My sobbing became broken whimpers that eventually bled into the silence of the car and the darkness surrounding me. The roads were pitch black and empty, and the thought of my car breaking down was horrifying, adding to my mounting fear. I turned on the music, trying to create a cocoon that would soothe my jagged emotions. About halfway through my favorite song, "Moon over Bourbon Street," the haunting notes began to lull my internal storm into perfect silence, as if I had entered the eye of the storm. In that moment, romance and soft feelings were stripped away, and the words struck a chord in me:

I was trapped in this life . . .
I can never show my face.

It was as though Sting was giving me a prophetic message of who I was quickly becoming. The darkness of the night became even more menacing. I popped the cassette out and hoped Jaye wouldn't ask to play it again. My favorite song was no longer my favorite; I couldn't bear to hear Sting's voice for a while.

Jaye stayed for the next four days. We didn't get into any more bad arguments, although it did get tense at times. On his last night with me, I lost track of time and left him at his hotel at 2:15 a.m., exceeding my curfew by more than three hours. The campus felt desolate, and only the parking lot lights were illuminated as I pulled into a spot. I ran from my car to the entrance of my dorm and yanked on the glass door. It was locked. There was a student at the security desk, and I waved to get his attention, mouthing, *Can you let me in?*

As he turned the lock and opened the door, I smiled. "Thanks so much . . . sorry to bother you." He looked at me with a strange expression but didn't say anything, which I thought was rude.

I am so ready for a good night's sleep. I got off the elevator on my floor; the hallway was quiet and dimly lit as I dug in my purse for my room key. Yet as I walked toward my room, I noticed light coming from under my door.

That's weird. I never leave my lights on. I turned my key in the lock and pushed the door open. When I walked into the room, the blood drained from my face. The dean of students sat perfectly straight on the edge of my bed, waiting for me. There were boxes stacked next to her. She looked at me with cold disapproval. "Chrissy, I'm sorry, but you are being dismissed. I've called your parents. It's very unfortunate, the decisions you've made, but you cannot continue your studies here anymore. Your father is expecting a call from you."

She sighed and walked out without a backward glance.

CHAPTER

17

I COULDN'T MOVE. The shock seized my voice, and I couldn't even let out a cry. My eyes swept through the room, and I began to shudder at how stark and bare it was. Everything had been stripped away from my walls, my dresser, my desk, my closet, and even my bed. The phone sat on a bare desk, and for the first time I was gripped by a fear of my parents because I had never been in trouble before.

What am I going to say to my dad? What is he going to say to me? My heart stuttered, beating hard in my chest as I slowly walked to the phone.

Taking a deep breath, I picked up the receiver and braced myself. My hand was shaking as I dialed my parents' number. Dad picked up on the first ring.

"Chrissy?" Hearing my dad's worried tone, I could imagine him hunched over his desk in the den, tears streaming down his face.

"Yes, Daddy."

"Your mom and I can't even . . . They called us, but why, Chrissy? How could you do this?" He was completely blindsided by what I had done.

My voice faltered. "I'm so sorry."

"They told us everything. We know you had that guy down there. What's his name, Chrissy?" The pain in his voice was like nothing I had ever heard. It was as if his worst fear had come to life and was clutching his neck, keeping him from breathing.

"Jaye." I was scared because I was exposed. I strained to hear his next words.

"I had a warning in my spirit about him, Chrissy. What was he doing down there? And what did you . . . ?" He stopped. At that moment, I knew what he wanted to ask but there was no way I could bring myself to say it out loud. "Why, Chrissy? Why? How long has this been going on? What have we done that you couldn't tell us the truth?"

My dad's strong voice was now broken whispers over the phone line. It was as if I had reached through the phone and punched him in the face.

"Daddy, I'm so sorry."

As soon as I said that, something rose up in me, and I was overcome by a need to defend Jaye, to make my dad understand. My words rushed out in a stream of tears, "But Daddy, it wasn't him . . . it was me! I promise! *I* made him come down. It was all *my* fault—"

"Listen to me . . ." Dad cut me off calmly and quietly, the protector in him rising up. The little girl in me who needed her dad obeyed. "Someone will be coming to pick you up and stay with you until Mom and I figure out what to do. Give your car keys to the person." His voice began to break again. "I have to go take care of your mom now. I'll call you in the morning."

He paused. I couldn't tell if he wanted to say more, then I heard, "Good-bye, Chrissy."

"Bye, Daddy, I'm—" The dial tone hummed in my ear as I whispered, "Sorry. I'm so sorry." His silence was heart-wrenching, and it broke me. I expected anger and even indignation for all the lies I'd told. I would have preferred that reaction.

The last thing I wanted to do was see my mom and dad suffer because of me. Pleasing them had always been the top priority of my life. But I loved Jaye. He had become my life. I needed him. *What's going to happen? Will they ever let me see him again? Will they ever let me out of their sight?* I faced the most difficult choice of my life: my parents or Jaye.

A battle raged inside me. On the one hand, the thought of hurting my mom and dad was devastating. I couldn't get the pain in my dad's voice out of my mind. I was causing them so much anguish, and yet I couldn't turn my back on Jaye. The conflict inside me was relentless, driving me nearly insane. I loved my parents, but I didn't want to change. In that moment, something cold encased my heart. I really didn't care who I hurt because I made my choice. I wanted what I wanted. I was going to be with Jaye, whatever the cost.

It was a whirlwind transition out of Bible college. Despite my parents' best efforts to provide for me, I defied them at every step. I believed my destiny was to be with Jaye so I took matters into my own hands. I found a woman in Queens who was willing to let me share an apartment with her until I could get on my own two feet. I contacted a temp agency, and soon after, I received my first assignment. Four weeks later, I was still at the same job and things couldn't have been better.

Walking up the steps from the subway station in Manhattan during the morning rush hour, I merged into the crowd of people making their way up and down Fifth Avenue. The mass of bodies streamed off into gleaming skyscrapers that grazed the clear blue sky. I felt an energy as I walked alongside people who looked like wealthy business executives. *Tap, tap, swish*—the tapping of high-priced shoes and the swish of expensive leather cases brushing against overcoats created a rhythm in my head that captured the mood of the morning frenzy.

I followed the numbers along the block until I finally arrived at my destination: 767 General Motors Building. Tilting my head back, I looked up at the structure stretching up to what seemed to be a mile high and across the whole city block. I pushed the glass revolving door and entered an enormous lobby with marble floors that led to elevators with gold-trimmed doors. People swept past me and squeezed into the packed elevators while I soaked up being in the middle of all the glamour. When I arrived at my floor, the elevator doors glided open and I stepped out. Poster-sized images of well-known models' faces on the walls framed the reception desk of the company where I worked.

Around midmorning, I glanced up from the report I was typing when I heard a door open. The executive walked out of her office and began talking to another executive in the hallway. I was amazed by her casually chic look, which had to have cost a small fortune. I straightened up in my chair as they approached my desk.

"Hey, how's it going?" She seemed genuinely interested in making sure I was fitting in with her team. "Were you able to finish that first document?"

I reached over and pulled a manila file folder from the stack on my desk. "Yes, here it is. I'm actually halfway through the second."

"Good work, Chrissy." She smiled and leaned her hip on the edge of my desk. "Well, now that you've blazed through your work, do you have any exciting plans this weekend?" I was pleased by her compliment and the special attention I was getting. We chatted for a few minutes, and then she disappeared into her office for a conference call. I was still stunned by where I was.

How in the world did this happen? And why me? When the temp agency said they had "just the place for me," I had no idea I would end up working for one of the largest cosmetic companies in the world: Estée Lauder.

Each day had been exciting so far, and this one was no different. The hours flew by, and I hadn't even noticed what time it was, until a stunning sunset filled the wall-to-wall window I could see from where I was sitting.

The executive's office door opened again, and she strolled out with her leather briefcase slung over her shoulder. "Hey, what are you still doing here? You're free to leave early on Fridays."

Trying my best not to seem overeager, I reached up and tucked a strand of hair behind my ear. "Really?"

"Definitely. And by the way, those bags on your desk are full of samples we want our employees to test before they are released. I hope you enjoy them." She smiled as she made her way to the elevators. "Have a good one! See you Monday."

"You too," I called out as she disappeared. I turned around and picked up the phone. I grew anxious with each ring, wondering why no one was picking up. My heart fluttered.

"Hello?"

I relaxed when I heard his voice. "Jaye, you'll never guess what happened today! A coworker told me that this isn't just a temp job, that they're actually considering me for a full-time position. Isn't this incredible?"

"Mhhmm. Yeah, that's great."

Why isn't he more excited for me? What is he doing?

"Well, anyway, what are you doing now? Where've you been today? What time do you want to meet?" He seemed distracted, which always made me feel like I needed to try harder.

"I had to take care of some things today," he said. "We can meet up later at your place."

My stomach tightened, and I began to feel more nervous.

"Maybe I can meet you now and we can grab dinner? I don't mind running errands with you." As I said good-bye, I quickly grabbed my coat and rushed to the elevator. At that moment, nothing else was more important than getting to him.

Over the next week I thought a lot about the possibility of working full time in the corporate headquarters of Estée Lauder. It would be a dream come true. But since Jaye worked evenings and the only time we could be together was during the day, I felt extremely uneasy. I was aware that passing over such an opportunity was crazy, especially since I was coming in without any experience or a degree. If I missed this big break, what hope did I have of all this happening again?

The office was buzzing on the following Wednesday morning since Estée Lauder's daughter company Prescriptives was releasing a fragrance that they hoped would take the industry by storm. I was still blown away that I was in the midst of the inner circle and privy to this kind of creativity. My love for all things fashion made what I was doing all day not seem like work at all. As I typed up the drafts that my manager gave me of each product's description, I considered myself part of the creative process for the very makeup that I used.

Pulling the last sheet of paper out of the electric typewriter, I saw two people out of the corner of my eye walking out of my manager's office. A few moments later, she peeked her head out and asked me to join her.

"Chrissy, have a seat." She was smiling from ear to ear, which was unusual—she was typically intense when it came to our work. "I am so excited about this. It is very rare when an opportunity opens up here for someone like you without any formal training. Well, hold on to your seat, because I am officially inviting you to be part of our staff. I am pleased to offer you a full-time position."

She reached over and handed me a contract with the terms of employment and my salary. "Congratulations, Chrissy."

"Umm . . ." I stammered and tried to find the right words. "I'm so sorry, but uh, I have some things going on in my life right now that are preventing me from being able to accept this."

Her smile disappeared and her eyes widened slightly. Conflicting thoughts raged in my mind. *What is going on in your life, Chrissy? What could possibly stop you from taking this? Then again . . . that's a lot of hours for him to be on his own. Do you really trust him? There are plenty of girls around this city. What will stop him from going out on you, from finding someone else?*

I thanked her for the generous offer, but that final voice had settled my decision. Two days later—my last day of work—I walked out of the GM Building resolved to sacrifice anything to remain close to Jaye.

It didn't take long for me to feel the stress of not having a job. I was desperately trying to hold things together as much as I could, seeing Jaye nearly every waking moment, but that didn't pay my rent. Over the previous few weeks, I hadn't been sleeping well and my constant fatigue was draining all my energy. I wasn't taking care of myself and didn't know what was going to happen. I was becoming more panicked by the minute because I knew time was running out for me. I had to do something.

One night, very late, I left the apartment for the corner phone booth; it was a dangerous neighborhood for a woman to be walking alone but I wanted to make this call in private. The area where I was staying wasn't short of characters, and the streets heated up at night. I was on the brink of crying, but I definitely didn't want to call attention to myself, especially when I passed a guy who didn't take his eyes off me all the way to the phone booth. I fumbled in my pocket for change, feeling extremely nervous about the phone call I was about to make. It had become obvious to me that I needed to go home.

I began to dial the number that represented my life before the current mess I had created for myself; just dialing brought a sense of peace to me, even though I wasn't entirely certain what response I would receive. "Hello, Dad?"

"Chrissy?"

"Yes. It's me. I was wondering if I could . . . just come home." After some tears and a series of empty promises, I was back in my room, surrounded by familiar things.

"Chris, are you hungry? I can make you something." My mom looked up when I walked into the kitchen.

"No thanks, Mom. I just want a little something sweet." I grabbed a Nestlé Crunch bar and bolted down the stairs to the sanctuary of my room. I had been living at home for a few months now, doing my best to maintain an illusion of normalcy. Taking a small bite and setting the candy bar on my dresser, I walked to the bathroom. A muted overhead light cast faint shadows on my face as I stood facing my bully, the mirror, waiting for it to tell me what to do.

Chrissy, your hair is perfectly set. Sculpted waves framed my face. Creamy foundation made a smooth, dewy canvas for the dark liner around my blue eyes, the dark purple making the creases deeper and a pale gold color highlighting the curve under my brows . . . *masterfully blended.* I applied bright pink blush to my cheeks and chose a mauve lipstick. *Well done.* The corners of my lips lifted in a small smile as my eyes scanned my face.

Yes. The mirror agreed. *You have a pretty face.* I breathed a sigh of relief.

But will it be enough? I gasped as the mirror went from compliments to condemnations. *Jaye loves your pretty face now. But what about your body? Will he love you when you grow bigger and bigger?*

My eyes widened, and I slowly looked down at the small bump peeking through my unbuttoned shirt. I wanted so badly to ignore it and pretend it wasn't there. I grasped the edges of my shirt, trying to quickly button it up.

It's not going to go away, you know. It's been four months—and you haven't told your parents? What exactly are you waiting for? What are you going to do? the mirror taunted. *What kind of magic do you have* now *that will keep Jaye with you?*

CHAPTER

18

WITH EVERY WEEK, my belly continued to grow and I tried harder to conceal it. When I had told Jaye that I was pregnant, I didn't get the response I expected. To me, he seemed indifferent to the news, which only fed my refusal to accept the truth. It was like I was a walking time bomb, and although an explosion would eventually come, I pretended the situation didn't exist. Somehow I convinced myself that being pregnant would just work itself out because the most important thing was for Jaye and me to stay together. And now, my need to feel good enough for him turned into desperation. I lived in denial that intensified as the baby grew within me, completely numbing me to reality. I had jumped back into church and family life to prevent any suspicion and as I got bigger, I wore larger, boxier clothing to camouflage my pregnancy.

I had a life growing on the inside, and at the same pace I was deteriorating on the inside and no one, including my family, knew. Pretending I was job hunting, I would sneak out to find Jaye, hoping his presence would bring me consolation. When we were together there was never any real talk about our future. The topic of marriage never came up. But that didn't stop me; I tried to be content with whatever I could get from him.

Jaye and I weren't going to nice restaurants and strolling hand in hand in Greenwich Village anymore. Rather, I was reduced to following him around wherever he was going, which made me crumble inside. I hurt so badly because now I had no strength to work to keep him. Although I had numbed myself to the fact that I was living in my parents' home and that my due date was growing closer and they were bound to find out, the tension I walked around with was maddening. I couldn't eat and I barely slept, and I couldn't tell a soul the reason why. There were moments when I was so stressed that I felt I would lose the baby for sure. Weeks went by, and then months. And yet I never once regretted coming home. The reason I returned was the same reason I agreed to get on a plane in February, when I was six months pregnant. To be with the person who had made me feel safe from the time I was a little girl.

It was 3:00 a.m. and dark in the huge plane, except for the faint glow of a few reading lights scattered here and there throughout the cabin. We had been in the air for hours and almost everyone was asleep. I had been awake for a while, enjoying the peace and quiet, when the pilot's voice announced over the loudspeaker that we were currently flying over the Andes en route to Buenos Aires. Nobody seemed to be paying attention but me. I was having a difficult time getting comfortable so I turned on the reading light and tried to finish the crossword puzzle that my dad had started, messing the whole thing up. I tucked the magazine and pen into the seat pocket when the flight attendant came by, smiled, and quietly asked, "Can I get you anything, miss?"

I pulled the blanket farther up and smiled back at her. "No, thank you." As she continued down the aisle I closed my eyes, wishing I could sleep, but I was feeling way too tense. It seemed that when I was most nervous, the baby moved the most. I slid my hands under the blanket and held my stomach. At least I was safe, and that's all that mattered. Leaning my head back, I glanced at my dad's profile while he slept. I grabbed the armrest to recline my seat some more and closed my eyes again. Soon I felt his hand on mine. Dad squeezed it three times.

For the next several days, under the starriest skies I had ever seen in my life, Dad preached at open-air camp meetings outside of the capital city, to a crowd who came from all across Argentina. After the services, we would all gather outside and eat together. Listening to the sounds of laughing families and broken English mixed with the soft tones of Argentinian Spanish made me forget about my own troubles for the moment.

Dad took every opportunity to show me off as he always did. The expression in his eyes reflected a sense of ease, as if nothing had changed between us, like time had stood still since the last time we had shared this experience together. Everyone treated me as they had when I had come there with Dad six years before, and that put me at ease.

At the end of a long week, Dad and I returned to Buenos Aires for our last day before heading home. He suggested that we go to the beach. I grabbed my swimsuit from my bag and put it on, adding a couple of layers over it.

"Chris, I got us a couple of chairs."

"Thanks, but I don't need one, Dad."

We found an empty spot where I laid out my towel on the hot sand and Dad set up his chair. As I got warmer and more uncomfortable, I began to peel off layers without thinking. I did cover my belly with a towel as I lay down on my back to soak up some sun. The warm breeze put me in a sleepy trance. The sound of children playing eventually woke me, and when I opened my eyes, all I could see was my belly sticking up in the air. I gasped, realizing that my dad, who was sitting beside me, was probably staring at it the entire time my eyes had been closed.

I quickly grabbed the towel and covered myself again. Only then did I peek up at Dad. His head was back and his lips slightly parted. He was fast asleep, exhausted from all the ministry he had done over the past few days. I sighed in relief, then turned onto my side with my back facing him. The fantasy I had created of a carefree life crashed into the reality of my situation.

I curled up into a ball, feeling the horror of how far my deception had gone.

Despite the scare on the beach, the trip gave me a time of rebonding with my dad. Our time together seemed to make way for some trust to be recovered, a new start for Dad and me. I decided to take advantage of that re-earned trust and ride on that wave when we returned so I snuck out to see Jaye more often. The more I saw him, the more the obsession grew. There was nothing I could do to get free of it—especially now that I was carrying his baby. When we were together, it often ended in fights, and more times than not, I'd be crying in public places. The fear of losing him, combined with my physical fatigue, was heightening my sensitivity to where his eyes wandered. Every woman with an hourglass figure who walked by became an immediate threat.

All day long, he was on my mind; the safety of the baby, never. I was so nervous all the time that I barely ate and I couldn't sleep. I kept telling myself, *It will all just work out*—my way of dismissing the fact that my due date was drawing near. I looked at my pregnancy as I would a common cold that would eventually go away. My parents could have really thought that things were turning around and that they were getting their daughter back, yet it was completely a ruse. Now entering the final trimester of pregnancy, I was becoming masterful at conning my parents and everyone around me.

At home and even at church, I noticed Mom starting to look at me in ways that made me wonder if she knew. If I saw her eyes scan me, I would suck in my belly and put on an extra layer of clothing, even though spring had begun and the temperatures were climbing. Those looks became more and more frequent, and I decided that I had better avoid her as much as possible. *Even if she suspects something, she'll dismiss the idea because of how crazy it is.*

It was a typical Sunday in early April when I ran across Flatbush Avenue, rushing back to church from Jaye's house, where I had spent the last several hours while Dad and Mom were in the early services. I dodged the moving traffic, focused on getting through the doors and slipping into the building unnoticed, before the third service ended. Figuring it would be best to avoid the balcony, I sat on the main level so that my parents hopefully would see me. As soon as I slipped into my seat, I could feel it—God's presence was so strong and evident in the room, it was undeniable.

Dad had the microphone in his hand and his eyes closed, while Mom took her place to direct the choir. I wondered what had been going on since the service started, because it seemed like there was a cloud over all of us. When I heard the intro to the song, I recognized it and knew that I had better brace myself to reject what was about to happen. As I slid down in my seat, the choir began to sing . . .

Jesus, He'll meet you where you are
Jesus, He heals your secret scars
All the love you're longing for is Jesus
The friend of a wounded heart.

As they belted out the final notes, the congregation stood and let out shouts of praise and applause to God. Dad then took the microphone and gently said, "I ask that everyone remain standing for a moment because I believe that God is already speaking to some people today. We don't have to wait for the end of the service to respond to God. If you felt the Lord reaching out to you today while the choir was singing and you need healing for your heart, I ask you to make your way to the altar, and we're going to pray for you."

A girl in the section to my right burst into tears and walked down with a tissue over her face, while dozens of people started coming down from the balcony. The area in front of the altar was so full that the aisles began to fill up with people intensely reaching out to God. Choir members came down from the choir loft and helped Dad pray. As the sounds of passionate prayers filled the room, I just stood there. I felt the pull on my heart as well, but I couldn't risk dealing with what I stood to lose if I gave in to God. Instead, I chose to remain a bystander at that moment, although I knew my heart had to be in the worst shape of anyone's in that room.

A few weeks later, I was talking to someone in the church lobby after the service when Mom's secretary tapped me on the shoulder. "Chrissy, your mom asked me to come get you. She's in the office."

"Okay, tell her I'll be there in a minute. I turned back to wrap up my conversation with the woman who had known me since I was a little girl, who was relentlessly inquiring whether or not I was still playing the piano. "So anyway, yeah, I'm not sure what I'm going to do next, but I still love fashion." As she went to hug me, I made it a short and quick side hug. I exited the lobby through a side door and walked around the building so I could avoid running into anyone else.

When I entered the office area, I asked the receptionist, "Do you know where my mom is?"

"She's in that office," she said, pointing to the door next to my dad's office.

I walked in, and Mom was sitting there alone. The vibe in the room felt strange to me as Mom told me to sit down. At first her voice was strong. "Chris, I need to ask you something." I could see that she was very shaky as she went on, and then her voice began to crack. "Chris . . . are you pregnant?"

I looked at the woman I had admired my entire life, who had always been the image of strength and beauty. Her shoulders were hunched over as if she'd lost all her strength. Beneath the beautiful clothes, she seemed fragile and almost broken.

In that moment, my world stopped, the breath knocked out of me. The fantasy I had created was shattered, and a million thoughts shot across my mind like a machine gun. *Their grandchild . . . I lied while I was living in their house all this time . . . Where will I go now? . . . What will the church say? I can't admit this . . . I can't hurt Mom like this . . . What will Jaye do?* I trembled, trying to think of a way out of answering her question. But all that came out was the shocking truth: "Yes, Mommy."

Her eyes welled up with tears and as one ran down her cheek, she asked, "How far along are you, Chrissy?"

Dropping my head, I answered, "I'm due in eight weeks."

CHAPTER

19

I HEARD THE PACING OF FEET above my basement bedroom. It went on intermittently throughout the night—1 a.m., 2:30, 3:45 . . . I couldn't sleep either, which wasn't unusual for me, except tonight I hoped that when I finally did fall asleep, I would never wake up again. I stared into the darkness, feeling like a stranger in my own bedroom.

After a silent ride home from church, gloom followed us into the house like an unwanted visitor. The look on my dad's face was unbearable for me to see; he couldn't bring himself to look me in the eyes. Mom was devastated too, yet I got the impression that she wanted to come with me to my room. But instead, she glanced at me from the staircase, her expression suggesting that she wished she could say more.

I must have finally drifted off, because the soft knock on

my door and Dad's voice—"Chris?"—startled me out of a deep sleep. I squinted at the clock: 11 a.m.

"Come in," I croaked hoarsely.

Dad stuck his head in. "Come upstairs when you can. Mom and I are in the living room and want to talk to you."

"Okay, give me a minute." He stared at me, then averted his eyes and quietly pulled the door shut.

As I swung my legs off the bed, a wave of dizziness and nausea swept over me. I took slow, deliberate steps to the bathroom sink, leaned over, and took a sip of water from the faucet before heading upstairs. As I opened the basement door into the kitchen, the atmosphere I felt in that empty kitchen was contrary to what I had always known.

When I walked into the living room, I found my parents just sitting there . . . waiting. Dad had been clutching his forehead with his hand but slowly lowered it to rest on the arm of the couch. He lifted his head and looked into my eyes. His eyes were red, like he had been crying a lot. I shifted my eyes quickly to Mom and noticed the utter exhaustion on her beautiful face.

She seemed to be studying me, reaching down deeply, trying to understand. Her gaze followed me as I made my way to the closest chair. Feeling weak and still dizzy, I slowly sat down. Even though I sensed that Mom wanted to be close to me, she moved closer to Dad with her hands in her lap.

Dad sighed heavily. "Chrissy, you know how much your mom and I love you, don't you?" His words opened a floodgate, and they both began to cry.

"Yes," I responded sullenly.

"Our hearts are broken, and we just don't know what to do.

We have done everything, tried everything. But Chrissy, the bottom line is that you have to decide what you want to do with your life now, because as far as we're concerned, you don't want help, you only want to tell us lies."

The blood rushed to my face. Steeling myself against whatever else they had to say, I braced for their decision.

"You know you're not the first girl in the church who's gotten pregnant," Dad said. "The pregnancy is not the huge problem we face. The problem is that our daughter, whom we don't recognize anymore, has become a compulsive liar and is obsessed with a relationship that's destroying her."

"Dad, it's not that . . . You don't understand."

"Well, help me to understand, Chrissy. You love this guy and he loves you?"

"Yes," I insisted, dropping my head.

"And you're carrying his baby? Well, where is he? Why isn't he taking any responsibility?"

I shouted back in my mind, *You don't know WHAT you're talking about!*

Dad continued, "Your life has become nothing else but sneaking around with him. You gave up college . . . you've given up your church, the people who love you . . . and you've been hiding in your own house with a life inside of you."

Dad's voice grew louder as he got up and walked toward me. "Chrissy, you won't let us help you! We can't help you because all you do is lie to us!"

I bit my tongue to keep from talking back. *I'm not a liar! You just don't understand!* I was barely holding back the turmoil building inside me.

Then I heard, "Mom and I spent the night talking and praying about what to do next. We want you to stay here with us but we know you will keep rushing back to him without thinking of the baby's welfare. Can't you see you're running yourself into the ground, Chrissy? We can't protect you, but we want to protect this baby—if you'll let us. There's a place in upstate New York that has been recommended to us where you can go. We'll take care of the arrangements."

I conceded; I had no strength left to argue and knew in my heart that I didn't have a strong argument anyway.

All I could see for miles out the window of the old beat-up station wagon were cornfields. The road was bumpy, and I was extremely uncomfortable. I tried to adjust my position to relieve the pressure on my back. My "hostess" looked over her shoulder and said, "We got another thirty miles to go. . . . You gonna be all right back there?" I stared at the wiry gray curls that covered her head.

"Oh, I'll be fine."

Her broad shoulders stretched the faded cotton dress that she was wearing, making the ugly rose pattern on it stand out even more. My eyes went back and forth between the Hanleys, the couple sitting in the front seat. *I'm not like these people, and I don't belong here.*

Even before we got to "the home," I determined not to let them get close to me. These people were not going to be my friends. I just wanted to get through the next few months and put all this behind me.

Mr. Hanley tried to ease the awkwardness, asking me about my flight. His wife gave me a pained smile.

In an attempt to not be totally rude, I commented, "I didn't know it was way out in the country like this. How long have you lived out here?"

We continued to make light conversation until we pulled up in front of a large old farmhouse. They led me across the porch, through a squeaky screen door, and into the kitchen, where I was introduced to four other girls who were all pregnant. I immediately felt like I had entered into a *program* instead of a *home*. The stark decor, the pamphlets, and the prenatal vitamins on the long kitchen table made the environment seem institutional.

"Chrissy, Lane will take you up to the bedroom. We'll be having dinner in an hour." Mrs. Hanley dug into the pocket of her dress, pulled out a pack of cigarettes, and headed out the side door.

Lane cleared her throat to get my attention. She smiled and asked, "Have you ever eaten venison?"

I gave her a puzzled look.

"It's deer meat."

"Uh, actually I haven't."

The girls all chuckled.

"Don't worry. You get used to it. Come on. Let me show you to our room."

I followed Lane through the living room, noticing the mismatched assortment of furniture. Nothing about this place felt like home, and the musty smell was already starting to cling to me.

As we climbed the stairs, I asked, "So will you and I be sharing a room?"

"Yes, but I won't be here for long; as you can see, I'm about ready to pop. The baby's due in three weeks or so. How about you?" We made our way down the hallway covered with dingy yellow wallpaper with faded blue flowers. Some of the edges were tattered and curled up, showing cracked walls beneath.

"I believe I'm due in eight weeks, but I'll know for sure tomorrow when I go to the doctor. They set up an appointment for me first thing in the morning."

"Wow—you're carrying incredibly small!" Lane said in surprise.

"Yeah, I guess I am." When we got to the room, she showed me which bed was mine and where to put my things.

"While you're getting settled, I'm going down to help get dinner ready. You must be worn out from traveling. Those country roads are enough to put you in labor!" I liked her sense of humor already.

"Don't forget to be down in an hour, okay, *dearie?*" she said as she winked and put two fingers above her head like pretend antlers.

I dropped my bags and sat on the edge of the twin bed that was assigned to me. Lying down and slowly stretching out, I felt really pregnant for the very first time. I took a deep breath and released it slowly, a wave of tiredness washing over me. I stared at my belly, actually seeing it for what it was. A few tears leaked out of the corners of my eyes and rolled into my hairline. I was so exhausted. My breaths hitched in my chest as I felt the little energy I still had slowly seep out of me. I was weighed down by a sorrow that I had never allowed myself to feel at home. It was as if the peaceful surroundings forced me to be still enough to finally rewind my life, something I had avoided over the past months.

No more entourage of friends . . . no more fashion . . . no more freedom . . . no more being made a fuss over . . . no more church princess . . . no more three hand squeezes . . . no more shopping trips . . . no more music that changed people. All the things that made me love my world, I had given up for this relationship. I thought about the insanity of getting and keeping Jaye, all the lies, pretending to be the "good girl," and trying to manage two opposing worlds. The burning desire to be the perfect couple with Jaye in my fashion-centered world warred with the girl who longed to be perfect in her parents' love-filled world. In the stillness of this unfamiliar place, the stark reality of my situation hit me. All this time, it hadn't been real to me, but as I lay there, I realized that I was going to have a baby, an actual person. Was I carrying a boy or a girl? It had never occurred to me to ask or even wonder before now. I rolled over on my side, tucked a pillow under my belly, curled up my legs, and let myself drift into a deep, dreamless sleep.

The clinking of silverware added notes to the side conversations and the soft murmurs of "Pass the venison," "Thanks," and "More peas, please."

"Girls," Mrs. Hanley chimed in, "tomorrow a lady from the local craft store will be coming to work with you on photo albums for your babies." Excited chatter drowned out the rest of her announcement as the girls talked about the last time they crafted. "Um, this time be sure not to glue the front pages shut, okay?" Everyone started to laugh. "Chrissy, have you ever crafted before?"

I looked up from my plate, wishing the food would disappear on its own. "Not really."

Lane laughed and said, "Well, this will be another new adventure for you."

"So, what do you think of the venison?" Mrs. Hanley asked.

"It's . . . different," I replied as I used the mashed potatoes and peas to cover up my helping. The voices droned around me as I glanced out the window and saw the fields stretching to the horizon. *How will Jaye ever find me here? Does he even want to find me?* I couldn't keep the thoughts from spiraling downward. *What is he doing and who is he with? I need to call him as soon as possible.*

"Mrs. Hanley, may I use the phone to call home?" I asked.

She paused from clearing the table with the girls and pointed to a door off of the living room. "Sure, it's right in there."

The jitters in my stomach calmed as I pushed away from the table and handed my plate to one of the girls on cleaning duty.

Hours later, while my roommate and the rest of the house were fast asleep, I tiptoed down to that room over and over again. At first, I called him every hour—with no answer. After several more attempts, I started dialing his number every half hour until someone at his apartment took the phone off the hook.

I slowly slid the handset down the side of my face, wincing at the jarring busy signal. Looking at the phone and then at my belly, I was overcome by all the things I had given up and how far I had fallen. I was tempted to run out of the house and hitchhike to the airport so that I could find him. Suddenly, the baby started to move, a reminder that something more than Jaye and me was at stake. I sat on the floor, leaning over with one arm holding my belly tightly and the other arm supporting me, until it buckled. I cried hysterically, feeling so betrayed.

It took a few weeks, but I finally began to warm up to the Hanleys. Even though I didn't think their house was nice and it annoyed me that we were out in the middle of nowhere, I grew to appreciate how they cared for all of us. Mrs. Hanley faithfully took us to our doctors' appointments, made sure we were eating well, and took each girl to the hospital when it was time to deliver her baby.

Lane had left after giving birth to a baby boy. I missed her good-heartedness and laughter. She had helped me adjust from the first day I arrived. We promised to stay in touch, and I hoped to visit her and the baby once they were settled. Right now, though, it was nice having a room to myself.

One afternoon when I was resting, Mrs. Hanley knocked on the door. "Chrissy, could you come with me to my office? I want you to meet Kathryn." I slipped on my shoes, and as I followed her down the hall, she continued talking. "You'll just love Kathryn. She meets with every girl who comes through our home. She's great at explaining the process and will answer any and every question you may have."

As we approached the office door, she stopped and laid a gentle hand on my shoulder. "Oh, and remember, you are not committing to anything by going to this meeting."

I smiled faintly. "Thanks, Mrs. Hanley."

When we walked in, Kathryn stood up and walked toward me. She smiled and her hazel eyes lit up as she brushed sandy brown hair away from her fair, slightly rounded face.

"Hello, Chrissy, it's so nice to meet you," she said, covering my hand with both her hands. Immediately, her warmth and friendliness put me at ease. Mrs. Hanley left the room and we made our way to the table. As Kathryn sat down and pulled her chair closer to the table, I admired her tailored tweed trousers and pretty blue blouse, complemented by a simple strand of pearls.

Step by step, she began to explain what her agency provided. She showed me a photo album of all the couples who were waiting to adopt a baby, pointing out their detailed biographies. I slowly turned the pages, examining every photo. These women appeared so ready, so eager to love, so prepared. All that I wasn't suddenly became magnified. I felt so incapable, so shattered, so distracted, so empty. *I'm not like any of them.*

Kathryn interrupted my thoughts. "You don't have to decide now. Another option would be to place the baby in foster care immediately after delivery, which allows you some time to make the decision that's best for you and the child."

I thanked her for her time and said that I had a lot to think over.

Reaching Jaye was hit or miss those days, but it only seemed to deepen my desire to be with him. When we did connect, we didn't come up with any real plans for what we would do when the baby was born. He couldn't afford to get us an apartment and I was not about to ask my parents for help because it would only prove that Jaye couldn't take care of me.

A week later, I knocked on the door to Mrs. Hanley's office. "Do you have a minute?"

"Sure, Chrissy, come in."

I walked over to her desk and laid down the papers I had been clutching. "After talking to Jaye, I've decided to sign the foster-care papers. Jaye said he would come for the baby's delivery but we know this is the right decision. Would you send the paperwork to Kathryn for me?"

She briefly scanned the papers and then raised her eyes to mine. There was a moment of silence.

Taking a deep breath, I said, "I know that this is the best thing."

CHAPTER

20

A SHARP PAIN TIGHTENED MY STOMACH and jolted me out of a deep sleep. *Could this be it? I need to get Mrs. Hanley.*

Everything happened quickly after that. Beads of sweat coated my face as I lay in the backseat of the station wagon, my feet pressing against the door with each agonizing contraction. *Are we there yet? Why does the hospital have to be so far away?* I clutched my round belly, closed my eyes tightly, and prayed that it would be over soon.

I don't remember much after we arrived at the hospital except bright lights, people rushing around, and intense pain. *I wish they would stop telling me to push. I am pushing!* There seemed to be a crowd in my room, but everyone blurred together. Gripping the railings on either side of the hospital bed, I gave one final push, lay back, and closed my eyes.

"It's a girl!" the doctor said.

Later that evening, the squeaking wheels of the portable cradle woke me. As the nurse entered my room, I was torn between wanting to see my baby and wanting her to go away because I was such a mess, feeling like such an unfit mother. I turned my head away.

"Here she is, ready to eat," the nurse said softly. I turned back as she handed the small bundle to me.

I don't want to look at her. Even though she was part of me, I know she wasn't anything like me. She was innocent and pure. The nurse gave me a bottle, smiled, and walked away. The moment I peeked at the tiny face, it was if a valve of my heart had been opened and was gushing out a torrent of uncontrollable emotions. My heart exploded with love, unlike anything I had ever experienced before. It was so strong that tears began streaming down my face. I could barely see her through the blur of my tears, but when I closed my eyes, her face was already imprinted in my mind. The sweet sounds of her gentle whimpers and her fast breaths going in and out drew me in. This was *my baby girl.* These were *her sounds.*

I pulled her closer to my face, and my first instinct was to hum a melody against her cheek, taking in the sweet smell of her skin. Alone with her in that dimly lit room, I reached over, still hurting from the delivery, and put the bottle in her tiny mouth. I couldn't stop staring at her. It seemed as though she was staring back at me. I never wanted this moment to end.

The sound of the door opening got my attention but didn't take me away from the rapture I was experiencing. As the nurse leaned over and gently took her from my arms, I watched her swaddle my baby to return her to the nursery.

For the rest of the evening, my mind was in a fog from pain medication. Finally I fell asleep, but in the middle of the night I awoke, disoriented.

Where am I?

I grabbed the metal bars on both sides of the bed and strained to pull myself up and reach for the privacy curtain separating the beds. There was no sound coming from the other side of the room, but I wanted to see if another patient was there. Every move I made sent sharp pains through my abdomen and a tightness from front to back.

After struggling for what seemed like hours to slide the curtain back, I was devastated when I saw an empty bed. I had hoped I wasn't alone, but I was. The television was tuned to a fuzzy channel with an old episode of *Perry Mason* playing. As I gingerly lay back down, I stared at the cracks on the ceiling. Thoughts jumbled in my head as I tried to make sense of everything that had happened. Then my heart was gripped with such a pang of loneliness that I closed my eyes; I couldn't bear it anymore. Eventually, I drifted off to sleep.

"They just called up from the lobby and said you have a visitor, miss," the nurse said as she yanked the cord to pull up the metal blinds, letting the bright midday light into the room.

"What time is it?" I whispered, semi-coherent.

"It's just past noon, and we will be bringing the baby in

shortly," the nurse replied. My heart jumped the moment she started talking about her. The memories of the previous night flashed before me as the nurse's voice interrupted my thoughts. "You'll be happy to know she had a great night and is responding well to the formula."

Even as the nurse spoke to me, I was still being carried away by this new feeling, an indescribable, overwhelming love that had been awakened when I really saw her for the first time.

"I'm so glad to hear that. When did you say you'd bring her to me?" I asked, longing to hold my baby again.

She stopped what she was doing and smiled at me. "Soon, I promise. We are also going to give you the papers to fill out for her birth certificate before long. Have you decided on a name?"

"Yes. I did this morning. Her name is going to be Susan Joy."

As the nurse opened the door to leave, I smelled perfume coming from the hallway and was startled by the distinct fragrance. My hands began to tremble as I set down my hairbrush. She walked into the room, closing the door quietly behind her. We were all alone, and our eyes locked.

"Hi, Chrissy."

"Mom, what are you doing here!"

She had an unsure expression in her eyes as she took halting steps toward my bedside. Our gaze held, and I silently sent her a desperate plea for the touch I had been missing. In an instant, I felt her arms around me and melted into the secure feeling of love, as she pulled me into a tight embrace and leaned into me.

"The Hanleys called and told us that you went into labor. *I needed to see you, Chrissy,*" she whispered in my ear. I squeezed her even tighter, wishing I could stay like this forever. My mom pulled away slowly and sat in the chair next to my bed. There was an awkward silence as she scanned the room. She pulled back, visibly uncomfortable at the condition of the room I was in.

For the first time I saw the pain and hurt weighing on her. As she looked out the window, I nearly cried out, broken inside at the thought of how much I loved and longed for my baby, and how much my mom must love and long for me. I knew what had compelled her to come.

"Here she is!" The nurse's cheery arrival was a blessing. She placed the little bundle into my outstretched arms. I pulled back the soft white blanket adorned with pale pink polka dots.

She's even more beautiful than yesterday. A thick cap of shiny, jet-black hair covered her tiny head, surrounding her rosy cheeks. Her heart-shaped lips pursed as she let out a small cry.

Mom almost jumped up from her chair, but controlled the urge. When she got beside us, she leaned down as she whispered, "Chris, she's so beautiful."

"I know, Mom. Isn't she?" I replied with childlike wonder.

Tears were welling up in Mom's eyes. She quickly turned away when she realized that I was watching her. Walking over to the window, she seemed to collect herself. I caught a pained look crossing her face.

The nurse came back in again with the paperwork for the birth certificate and handed it to me. As she began to give me further instructions, Mom hastily came back over to the bed. Wrapping her hands around my face, she drew me close and pressed a kiss into my hair.

Her voice broke as she whispered, "I love you, Chrissy." And then with a pleading tone, she said, "Please call Dad and me as soon as you're discharged from the hospital, okay?" And then she was gone.

Something told me that she needed to leave because she was going to completely break down. I could picture her rushing through the halls of the hospital trying to race to the security of her car, where she could let all of her emotions out.

The nurse had been watching the whole exchange and now lowered her eyes back to the paperwork. "I'll just give you some time to finish this up, and I'll come to put the baby down in about an hour."

My discharge from the hospital crept up on me without me realizing it would actually happen. I was so caught up in the euphoria of giving birth that I forgot about the fact that I had to leave. Opening the bathroom door, I snapped shut my makeup case and eyed my overnight bag in the corner of the room. As I picked it up and laid it on the bed, I stood there, preparing myself to face my old clothes with my new body. With some reluctance, I unzipped my bag and pulled out the outfit I had packed, my favorite jeans and a semifitted shirt. I dreaded what came next: Would I fit into them now? And how would I look?

Slowly, I slipped one leg and then the other into the jeans, pulled them up, and zipped them effortlessly. I was ecstatic; I couldn't believe how easily I fit into my regular clothes! I walked over to the mirror and did a slow turn. The hospital scale next to the door beckoned me. "Come on over here . . . You know you want to." I hurried over and stepped up, adjusting the balancing weights on the bars. Each time I moved the balance down a notch, the smile on my face widened: 118 pounds!

Suddenly, it was the old me again. No more hiding my belly and no more struggling to find something concealing to wear.

I imagined myself walking in Greenwich Village with Jaye, once again dressed to perfection, with all eyes on me. I stepped off the scale and went back over to the mirror. It had been a long time since I had done a 360 and felt this good. My body actually looked *better* in my opinion. It seemed more womanly and curvy.

Perhaps he will look at me with fresh eyes because I am even more appealing with this new body. At that moment, I felt like a switch flipped inside me, my focus changing from motherhood back to Jaye. I was desperate to capture and keep his affections. My longings for Jaye consumed me once again.

A brisk knock on the door snapped me out of my daydream. A social worker walked into my room with a small stack of papers in one hand and the other extended toward me in a greeting.

"Hello, Chrissy, I am the baby's caseworker. I wanted to go over some final details before you leave."

I began arranging things in my overnight bag, trying to distract myself with something. It was unlike me to not make eye contact with someone who was speaking to me. But this time I couldn't bring myself to do it; being polite did not take precedence at the moment. I began to play with the zipper on the bag, mindlessly pulling it back and forth. I could feel her getting closer to me, but she didn't force herself on me, and I was glad. Her voice softened, in what seemed like an effort to defuse the tension. "We have a really special family prepared to pick up the baby in about an hour. It's a great placement, Chrissy." She paused, giving me a chance to respond.

I didn't say anything.

After a minute or two, she came around the bed and gently grasped my arm to try to connect with me.

"Chrissy?"

I continued to avoid her eyes and slightly turned to stare at the hands holding my arm.

"Are you okay?" she asked, the concern rising in her voice. "Listen. It's my responsibility to ask you again. You seem uncertain. Are you still sure you want to put your baby in foster care? It's not too late to stop the process if you've changed your mind."

When Jaye came for the delivery, I was secretly hoping that he would have a solution. That he was going to say, "Let's keep the baby. I have an apartment for us." But he didn't.

My mind was swirling with all the reasons that had initially convinced me to sign the papers. *I won't be able to handle this. I have no money and can't take care of her.* Then another reality struck me. *How do I tell my parents that I need their help, because clearly Jaye isn't going to help me?* Resigned, I looked at her for the first time. "Yes. I am sure. I understand everything you said." I picked up some more items and put them in my bag. She looked at me for another moment and quietly walked out of the room.

A short time later I stood in front of the hospital, waiting for the Hanleys to pick me up. As a warm breeze rustled my hair, I stared at nothing in particular. I had reached a crossroads and chosen the path that seemed best. I simply shut down my feelings and walked away.

CHAPTER

21

THE HEAT OF THE SUN PENETRATED the scratchy bedspread I pulled over my head to block out the light. With my body curled in a tight ball facing the wall, I couldn't help but wonder why Mrs. Hanley hadn't warned me. Every part of me hurt. My heart ached as if it had been ripped out and battered, over and over. My body throbbed, as though I could still feel the pain of delivery that most mothers forget with their baby beside them. My chest felt like I was being pressed into the bed and I couldn't breathe. My breath escaped between broken cries, but I didn't want to breathe because I didn't want to live anymore. No one told me that these would be the darkest days of my life.

It had been three days since I had been discharged from the hospital. I managed to numb myself to the most difficult thing I'd ever had to do. Even though living in denial was something

I had gotten really good at, it started to wear off the moment I got back to the Hanleys' house. They told me I could remain at the home until I could figure out what I wanted to do next—I guess that was nice of them. Lying in the same bed that was assigned to me the day I arrived, I suffered alone while my baby was in someone else's arms.

The bedroom became an isolated cave where I hid away because I couldn't bear being around people and I certainly didn't want to talk about anything. Besides, there was nothing to talk about. I had made the decision in the first place because I couldn't decide how I felt about giving up my baby for adoption and needed time to think. *The Hanleys are downstairs probably thinking that I'm resting, giving my body a chance to recover and doing some soul-searching.* I wasn't doing any of those things. For the past three days, from sunup to sundown, I had been upstairs suffering, as if I were mourning my baby's death.

And then I just knew . . .

I went running down the stairs, the decision made. I didn't have anything actually figured out, but it didn't matter. My daughter belonged with me, in my arms—immediately. Every girl in the home, including me, knew that they couldn't live there with their babies. But I would sort that out later. Right now, the best thing for Susie was to be with me.

When I told Mrs. Hanley what I planned to do, her response seemed emotionless. We were alone, sitting across from each other at the dining room table. I leaned in closer to her, my voice shaking. "I know you may think this is crazy because I don't know how to do this, but you have to understand—I have no choice!"

Mrs. Hanley pulled back from the table and sucked in her breath, as if she were trying to stop herself from saying what she really wanted to say. Then in a gentle voice, she replied, "Chrissy, when was the last time you talked to your parents? Don't you think you should call them? Girls come through this place from such difficult situations—no family, no support. But you . . . you have an incredible family who loves you. They want to—"

I cut her off. "I'm not going to do that. You wouldn't understand."

Without delaying another moment, I ran up to my room to begin packing. I grabbed my suitcase and tossed it on the bed. The few things I had brought with me when I first came two months before were in the bottom drawer of the worn dresser that Lane and I had shared. Grabbing what was there, I threw it into the open suitcase along with the items that hung in the closet. It felt good to be leaving, and although I would never forget that room because of the nightmare of the last three days, it was also the room where I had first felt my labor pains.

Placing my makeup case and hair supplies on top of the packed clothes, I looked at the clock sitting on the bedside table. A flashback of that first moment of labor came to me. It had been 4:23 a.m. when I had felt that first twinge, never expecting it to be "the one" since it was eight days before my due date. I remembered being kind of afraid, yet feeling like I was going to be a hero of sorts very soon just because I would be delivering a baby. Now my job was to be a hero, to rescue and reclaim my daughter. I slammed the suitcase shut and snatched it up. Leaving the room a mess, I bolted down the stairs.

"Mrs. Hanley!" I called out. "Mrs. Hanley, I'm ready!" I was frantic to get in the car and leave. I saw Mr. Hanley sitting at the kitchen table. "Where is she?" I pleaded, trying to catch my breath.

"She's already in the car, Chrissy," he said, the worry on his face evident. Dashing past him without a good-bye, I headed for the front door and swung it open. *Thunk . . . thunk . . . thunk.* I dragged my suitcase behind me down the porch steps and across the lawn and dirt road to the station wagon. I tossed my suitcase in the back, jumped in the passenger seat, and yanked the car door shut. The look on my face must have been enough of a signal to Mrs. Hanley to step hard on the gas pedal. As the tires kicked up a cloud of dust, she said nothing and I said nothing.

We were silent for the next half hour before pulling up to what appeared to have once been a large, stately brick farmhouse. Not waiting for Mrs. Hanley, I raced up the front steps and knocked on the edge of the worn screen door. An older, simply dressed woman appeared and with one look at my face, stepped back to let me in. She pointed to a room off the main entryway, with the door slightly ajar. I hurried in, barely noticing the gaudy pink paint and the shabby crib that held the most precious thing to me: my baby. I gasped as her beautiful eyes stared up at me. At that moment, I was enraptured, in total bliss. Yet an uneasy feeling surfaced: If I didn't immediately escape with her, she might be taken from me. I lifted her out of the crib, put her face against my chest, and quickly left. By the time Mrs. Hanley walked out of the house, Susie and I were already settled in the backseat of the car.

Once again Mrs. Hanley said nothing and I said nothing.

After a few minutes, though, I noticed her glancing at me in the rearview mirror. I didn't want to talk to her about the next steps or even how I was feeling at that moment. Perhaps attempting to fill the awkward silence, she turned on the radio. As the music played and the car rocked over the uneven dirt road, my baby's eyelids became heavy and she blinked slower and slower until she was lulled to sleep.

I stared at her and began sobbing silently. At first, they were tears of joy that came from the too-good-to-be-true feeling that we were together again and that she was all mine. But they slowly turned into sorrow-filled tears as I began to feel like I was suffocating. I became plagued with thoughts of how I had treated her to this point, how helpless she was, how much she depended on me, and how weak a person I was. I loved Susie so much and was desperate for her to understand the depth of all I felt for her. But part of me knew that if she were old enough to understand, she could wonder: *Does my mom really love me? She tried to give me away—would she do it again? Why did she conceal me for all those months? Was she ashamed of me?*

Getting hold of my emotions before I beat myself up any more, I quietly murmured, "I can do this." My resolve was so strong and I felt laser focused, determined to make everything up to her. *With* Jaye or *without* Jaye, I knew I couldn't live without *her*. But I also knew that I wanted Jaye. I was convinced that he was the one who was supposed to love not just me, but our daughter.

Ever since I had been a little girl, I had imagined belonging to a man one day, and Jaye became that man. I gave him my heart and I gave him my body and now we had a child together.

Even though I knew I did a lot of things wrong, why couldn't my dream still come true? Why shouldn't this work out, and why shouldn't we try? Why should I just walk away?

"Chrissy?" Mrs. Hanley raised her voice over the music, interrupting my thoughts. "Chrissy, dear, where exactly am I taking you?" She started talking as if she couldn't help herself. "I . . . I really do wish I could take you, well, both of you, but . . . I . . ."

Suddenly, she stopped and her expression closed up. "So where does Lane live now?"

I pulled a tiny address book from my purse and rattled off the address of my former roommate. When I had called her that morning, explaining what had gone on at the hospital and over the last few days, Lane had invited me to stay with her for a little while until I could get back to Jaye.

Lane didn't have much but she generously made room for Susie and me in her tiny apartment. Her boyfriend was supporting her so she couldn't really help me financially. She did whatever she could to make life a little easier for me, such as driving me to appointments and to the grocery store. Jaye visited me and the baby during the couple of months I was with Lane and would stay a few nights. Each time he returned to Brooklyn, he left me lonelier than the time before.

The weather was dismal and the gray of the sky was drizzling into my heart. Lane pulled her beat-up car into an empty space at Tops Friendly Market and parked. It had been two weeks since Jaye's most recent visit, and before we headed inside the store, she broached the subject. "So, Chris, I was wondering what your plans are. I mean, when did you say Jaye is going to get a place for you?"

Without hesitation I replied, "Oh, I'm so sorry. I know I said I'd be gone by now. Jaye didn't exactly say he was getting a place for me, but don't worry. I was actually thinking of heading back to New York City in the next few days."

"It's not that I'm trying to rush you, Chrissy, it's just that I have company coming and . . ." I could tell she was flustered and a little embarrassed about asking when I would be leaving. She was also probably annoyed that Jaye had already come to visit twice and I wasn't contributing anything toward rent or living expenses.

"No, really, Lane, it's not a problem. Jaye is waiting for me in New York," I told her as I struggled out of the car with my precious baby in one arm and swinging the strap of my purse over my other shoulder. "I shouldn't be long in the store," I said, closing the car door gently with my knee.

The bright fluorescent lights and the cold air coming from the frozen-food section made me cover Susie's head with her blanket and hold her tighter to my chest. Up and down the aisles I yanked the cart around with one hand, my stomach churning the entire time. *I am so hungry.* Cravings for the foods and snacks I loved the most began to spike, yet I knew not to grab anything that wasn't itemized on the paper in my pocket.

I stood there staring at the cookies and felt like taking a pack and hiding it under the two diapers in my purse. Even though the lady coming down the aisle was clearly looking for something on her shopping list, I couldn't help but imagine she was coming for me and was going to confront me for contemplating shoplifting.

I pulled aside for a second to pull out the paper again while rocking the baby to sleep. The list seemed meager, even though the woman who had registered me with WIC said that it would be enough to keep the baby and me healthy.

As I walked by the meat section and passed items that my mom always had in the fridge, I indulged in self-pity for a moment. Lane was waiting in the car and I didn't have much time, so I just grabbed cheese, bread, and formula, then made my way to the cashier. I could feel the eyes of a well-dressed woman standing behind me as I pulled the vouchers out to pay for the food. Glancing back at her, I saw her pursed lips and the way she looked down at me with disgust. I felt my cheeks get warm as I continued to check out, wishing I could be anywhere but here, settling for less than the basics so my baby and I could just survive.

It was a warm early summer day in Brooklyn when I walked up the steps of the old brownstone with my daughter in my arms. I was nervous and uneasy because of the sounds coming out of the apartments as I made my way up. A smoky haze hung in the hallway, and TVs and stereos were blaring. I could already hear loud talking carrying down from the top floor where I was heading. As much as I didn't want to be there, I wanted to be with Jaye.

After several knocks I walked in without a welcome. It was the furthest thing I had ever experienced from my idea of home, but this is where Jaye came from and where he stayed—ten blocks from my church and the wonderful world that I had walked away from.

I sat on the vinyl couch with the sounds of cars passing by, holding our baby with no supplies to care for her . . . simply a blanket.

I needed Jaye. I would just wait on that vinyl couch for him with our baby in my arms, hoping that when he got home he would be happy to see me.

CHAPTER

22

THE STRESS AND EMBARRASSMENT of staying at Jaye's house was unbearable. I didn't know his family that well, and now I found myself living with Jaye, his parents, and his younger sister in their one-bedroom apartment, eating their food and taking up their space. Simple things like taking a shower were so awkward, and it seemed as though our intrusion was impeding their desire to get know me. Since there really wasn't any bedroom free for the baby and me, we both ended up sleeping on the couch—yet I was fine with that, since that meant I would be across the room from Jaye, who slept there on another couch.

With each passing day, I was reminded that I was breaking my promise to be the kind of mother my baby needed and deserved. Here I thought that I could take care of Susie on my own, but I couldn't even get her a crib to sleep in. The weight of guilt about my baby felt like two hands clutching my shoulders and pressing me down; I could not get out from under that feeling.

As if the guilt alone wasn't enough, my fear was even greater. I was so afraid that I was no longer *that girl* Jaye found captivating and special. Every time he left for work, he seemed so detached—and I felt so abandoned. In the darkness of the night, staring at Jaye sleeping on the second couch always made me more determined to get things back to when they were good. I refused to believe that my relationship with him wasn't going to work. Yet deep in my heart I knew there wasn't much glue to hold us together, not even our daughter.

Things were very tense between us most times, despite the fact that every time we had a chance to be alone, we were intimate. What was so demoralizing was that despite how physical our relationship was, it wasn't making him closer to me at all. Whenever we were intimate, I felt cheap and used because I wasn't getting what I was looking for in return. I really believed that giving myself to him would seal our connection, but it didn't. Every time I was hopeful, but I was left with more and more hopelessness.

One morning I woke up with the realization that the light had completely gone out of my life. The world I loved as a child was not my world anymore. Hugs and kisses, love and admiration, people who adored me—it all seemed so far away. Outside the window of that Brooklyn brownstone, the Sunday morning sun shone brightly. But Sundays didn't have much significance any longer. Today was like any other day, yet for some reason I couldn't help but think about the Brooklyn Tabernacle and the fact that it was just blocks away. I wanted so badly to be there, yet I was trapped by my own obsession. I missed my parents so much, but being close to them just didn't seem to be an option. I had no alternative at this point other than to stay, even if it meant following a man around, content with the crumbs of his affection.

Later that morning, Jaye and I got into an argument, as we often did. As it escalated, I began to hit a desperate low and found myself extremely vulnerable, probably more vulnerable and hurt than I had ever felt with him. Mid-argument, Jaye left the apartment, seemingly drained by my inexhaustible need for him to prove that he really loved me and that I was still the only one in his life. The quiet click of the closing door was like a loud bang that reverberated in my ears, making me double over as if I had been punched in the gut.

"No! Wait!" I started toward the door to stop him, but the pain of all that had been said and left unsaid kept me fixed in one spot, alone and rejected. I stumbled over to where I had tried to create a safe little haven for my baby, surrounded by pillows in one corner of the couch. Toppling over, with whimpers that turned into wailing, I pressed my face into the vinyl cushion and gripped it with my nails, digging in, trying to tear it. At that moment, I had nothing left.

Susie started crying, but I couldn't comfort her because *I* needed to be comforted. I had nowhere to run and no one to turn to. I don't know how long my face was pressed into the cushion while I bawled like a baby. When my tears died down, I slowly pulled my face away from the vinyl. I was in such despair that for the first time I really wanted to find someone I could go to for solace.

My swollen eyes tried to focus. *I need to call Al.* It made perfect sense. Though we hadn't talked in a while, he was the only person I called sporadically and confided in since disappearing from the church. *He knows Jaye and he knows me. He'd understand.*

I picked up the phone and began dialing, calling the friend that both Jaye and I had deserted. *Ring, ring . . .* As the phone rang, I wondered how he would receive my call. I had so abruptly ended our friendship in pursuit of his friend. On the fourth ring, his mom answered in a heavy Spanish accent.

"Hello, Maria? This is Chrissy. Is Al home?" I waited, hoping so badly that he was there.

"Oh, *sí*, Crissee, *espera, por favor.* Albert!" Her voice rose over the lively Latin music playing in the background.

"Sí, Mamí. Un momentito."

I had a sudden attack of nerves as I waited for him to pick up the phone.

"Hello?" he said in the recognizable deep tone.

"Al, hi. It's me, Chrissy."

"Chrissy! How are you?" Hearing a familiar voice was so soothing, like a touch of home for just an instant.

Trying to hold back more tears, I answered, "I'm close by and . . . I was wondering if I could come over?"

"Sure." I could tell he was surprised but he added quickly, "It would be great to see you, Chris."

"Okay, just give me a few minutes and I'll be there." As we hung up, I breathed a sigh of relief because he asked no questions. Running downstairs, I handed Susie to Jaye's older sister, who lived in the apartment below, telling her I would be back in a little while.

Walking toward Al's house, I glanced down at myself and took stock of how I looked, trying to imagine what he would see. My flat, mostly concave stomach and belly button were exposed below my short black midriff shirt and above my faded khaki green balloon pants. Al was used to seeing me dressed nicely, and now I looked run down and shabby. When he saw me, I figured that he would notice I was much thinner than even before my pregnancy. But would he suspect that it was because of a poor diet and my living conditions? Slipping through behind someone at the front door of the apartment building who had been buzzed in, I began climbing the five flights of stairs. A surge of excitement came over me as I grew closer to a piece of my old life, but the trek up the steps was exhausting.

He must have been watching for me from the window because I heard him calling down the hall, "Chris?"

I walked toward the sound of his voice and was so pleased to see him.

He leaned over and gave me a quick hug, smiling as though he were sincerely happy to see me too. "Come inside. Are you hungry?"

I noticed his eyes taking in my appearance and then he got a weird look on his face. I was slightly embarrassed at how unkempt I was. But those thoughts vanished as soon as I stepped into the warmth of the apartment, feeling a peace I had not experienced in a long time. I was just around the block from Jaye's place, in the same unsafe neighborhood, yet this felt like such a refuge. The clean and orderly living room had little porcelain figurines that sparkled, and the aroma of Cuban food filled the house, making it incredibly welcoming. We sat down to talk, and he spoke kindly to me, which served to calm my nerves. I wondered if Al could tell that I was extremely embarrassed about the way Jaye and I had deserted him, but if he did, he didn't show it.

He seemed to pick up right where we had left off and began to fill me in on church life and some of my old friends. I could tell that Al was being very careful not to pry, giving me a chance to talk since it was unclear why I was even there.

After listening shyly for a few moments, I suddenly broke in. "Has my dad said anything about me to the church? Al, what do they know?"

"Actually, he hasn't said a word, but . . ." Al paused, dropping his head. Then he looked into my eyes. "Chris, I've seen your dad crying. He's called me into his office, asking if I knew how you were doing or where you were. I've seen him so broken right before having to walk into one of the services, and then somehow he would still preach his heart out. It's painful to watch him go through this, but I can tell God is really close to him."

Squirming in my seat, I abruptly changed the subject. "So, do you miss baseball?" I remembered how much he loved playing from our conversations when we had first met.

"No, not really." Looking at me with concern, he asked, "How's Jaye? I haven't talked to him in so long."

"He's . . . okay, I guess. He's still working in that print studio. You know what? I need to go—he's probably wondering where I am."

Al frowned for a second but quickly agreed. "Okay, I'll walk you down."

By the time we got downstairs, it was like we had that "old friend" connection again. He pushed the heavy black wrought-iron security door and held it open as I stepped out of the building. We stood there chatting for a few minutes when Jaye suddenly appeared. Not knowing how he would respond, I stayed quiet.

"What's up, Al," he said, clipping the words.

"Hey, what's up, man!" Al greeted him cheerfully.

There was an awkward silence, and then Jaye said, "Chris, we need to get back to the baby."

Under my breath, I said a quick good-bye to Al and followed Jaye down the block. I could feel Al watching us, but I didn't dare look because Jaye was fuming. He thought I had "put our business out there," and even though I denied it, he didn't want to hear it.

The days and then weeks to follow were so stress-filled that my body actually began to break down. Between juggling to give Susie what she needed and trying everything possible to hang on to Jaye, the little physical strength I had was gone. The way I was living was what I considered "lowlife" and yet I was trapped by my own longings.

It was a sticky July afternoon in uptown Manhattan when I slowly climbed up the stairs from underground onto Columbus and 59th Street. The subway let me off only a few blocks from my first temp agency appointment, and I had made it into the city with plenty of time to spare. I was feeling light-headed and weak, as if I were coming down with some kind of flu bug. I dismissed it, figuring it had to be because of the heat. Looking for the closest bench to rest for a moment, I checked my watch.

I was dressed heavily for a hot summer day, but I knew it was my best attempt at getting the corporate appearance my interviewers would be looking for. Still dragging down the street, I found another bench and nearly collapsed on it. Trickles of sweat ran down my back.

As I stared down at the ground, I spotted a kid pouring his drink into the grate on the sidewalk. I knew time was slipping away from me, just like that drink. It became clear that I was going to miss my appointment and that something was wrong when I began to shake from chills rushing through my body.

"Excuse me, sir," I said to a businessman sitting next to me who was drinking coffee out of a Styrofoam cup. "Do you know where the nearest emergency room is?"

He leaned forward and pointed to the right. "It's a few blocks that way. Do you need help?"

"No, I'll be okay." I got up slowly, gasped, and gripped my side as a needlelike pain shot through me. "I'm . . . I'm sure I'll be fine. I'm sorry. Which way did you say?"

I walked at a snail's pace toward the hospital, feeling as though I was chained to a load that I was hauling down the street—the anxiety of going one more day without any money.

The emergency room at Roosevelt Hospital was chaotic and full of all kinds of characters when I walked up to the desk to check in.

"May I help you?" the nurse said without looking up from her paperwork.

"I'm feeling severe pain in my—"

She abruptly cut me off. "Insurance card, please?"

"Uh . . . I don't have one," I stammered.

"Well, sign in here and just wait for your name to be called."

Several hours later, I lay in a hospital bed, hooked up to an IV that was pumping me with antibiotics, diagnosed with a severe kidney infection.

An older doctor came into my room and closed the door behind him. Picking up my chart, he peered over his reading glasses. "Miss Cymbala, I am concerned about your condition. Have you, by chance, been suffering from urinary tract infections? Your condition wouldn't have become this severe unless you neglected other symptoms."

I looked up at him sheepishly. "Yes, I have. But I thought I was getting better."

He sighed and closed the chart. "Well, you seem pretty run down, and you need to understand that a kidney infection can develop into something very serious. We're going to take you down for some more tests soon. For now, just rest and let's see how you react to the medication in the next couple of hours."

When the doctor left the room, I couldn't help but close my eyes and rest.

I woke up suddenly and realized I had not called Jaye. "Hey, I'm in the hospital. They said I have a kidney infection." As I went on, it was evident that Jaye was in the middle of something at work.

"Chris, where's the baby?"

"She's with your mom."

He let out a frustrated breath. "You can't leave her there—I've told you that. I can't get off work right now. Let me try to get this done and leave as quickly as I can."

I was torn between feeling hurt and anxious. Hurt because he didn't seem to care that I was sick and anxious because I didn't want him to be mad at me. "Okay," I said with a small voice.

After hanging up the receiver, I lay there feeling incredibly weak, wondering why I was so unable to defend myself or even fix things. Just when I thought I had hit rock bottom, I found myself sinking deeper into a pit. I felt abandoned, but not only by Jaye. I had abandoned myself—allowing my obsession to strip me of feeling worth anything more than I was getting.

Barely able to pick up the phone again, I grabbed the receiver and dialed.

"Hello?" Al answered on the second ring.

"Hey, Al? It's me, Chrissy."

My voice shook, as I held myself back from bursting into tears. "I was wondering if you could do me a big favor . . ." Embarrassed but frantic, I appealed to him. "Would you go to Jaye's apartment and get my baby for me and bring her to the city? I'm so, so sorry to bother you, Al."

I tried to rush on before he could interrupt me. "I know this may sound kind of bizarre, but I really need you to bring her to the hospital. I'm here at Roosevelt Hospital. You know, by Columbus Circle?" Another wave of pain hit me in my back, and I swallowed hard to keep talking. "When you arrive, just ask for my room number, okay? Thank you so much, Al. I really appreciate this. See you soon." I had to hang up quickly because I felt like I was going to faint.

For the next couple of hours, I did anything I could to pass the time while I waited for Al to come with Susie. I turned on the TV, but instead of distracting me, the sound became irritating, so I turned it off. Seeing my purse slightly opened, I grabbed the mirror and noticed how my sickly, pale complexion was making the dark circles under my eyes even more prominent. I snapped my purse shut, closing my eyes tightly and trying to breathe through the gnawing pain in my side. I felt dizzy from fever and kept trying to clear my vision so I could see the clock on the wall.

I wonder what's keeping Al? My stomach grumbled, and I remembered that I hadn't eaten all day and there wasn't any food close by. Between the hunger pangs and the pain from the infection, I couldn't get comfortable enough to take even a quick nap.

Finally, Al walked in with my baby bundled in a light pink receiving blanket. Too weak to sit up, I tried to shift on the bed but fell back weakly.

"Thank you so much, Al. You must think I'm crazy." He laid Susie in my arms, careful not to disturb the tubes connected to the IV.

His face was flushed as he said, "I've been so worried. What happened, Chrissy?"

I didn't want to get into all the details with him. "It's probably nothing, but they're still running more tests."

Changing the subject, I interjected before he could follow up with more questions, "How did you get here?"

His face became more flushed. "I took the subway. It wasn't so bad. Actually, the hardest part was getting past the nurse's station with a baby."

I smiled, thinking of him rushing through New York crowds, carrying a baby.

He paused, and I knew he was going to ask me what I still hadn't figured out yet. "Chris, what can I do for you? What are you going to do now?"

I held my daughter tighter and lied again to my friend. "Oh, don't worry. It will be fine. Jaye will be here soon. I really appreciate this. I don't want to keep you any longer. Seriously, we'll be just fine."

He looked doubtful, then let out a sigh. "Okay, Chrissy. Call me if you need anything." He said an awkward good-bye and then left.

I looked down at Susie, and my heart skipped a beat when I heard a nurse's cart wheel by, fearful that the staff would find her in here. I knew what I needed to do. I flipped the sheets back, carefully swung my legs over the side of the bed, and set her in the middle of the bed. I gingerly stepped into and pulled up my dress slacks. I gritted my teeth, removed the tape that held the IV needle in place, then yanked the needle out. Quickly dabbing the few spots of blood on my hand, I slipped into my shirt, buttoned a few buttons, and put on my blazer.

I picked up the baby and rocked her for a minute, trying to make her fall asleep. Cracking the door open, I checked to make sure the way was clear. I snuck to the closest stairwell and labored down each flight of stairs. With the last drop of adrenaline I had, I pushed open an emergency exit and escaped into the night.

CHAPTER

23

THE NEXT FEW MONTHS BEGAN ANOTHER CYCLE of craziness for Susie and me. Out of sheer desperation, I called my parents because I just didn't know what else to do. They asked me if I was ready to walk away from my toxic relationship. At that point, I was willing to agree to anything.

"Yes, Dad. I want to get things right for me and the baby. I'll listen to what you and Mom say, I promise."

Through my parents' contacts, I got an incredible opportunity in Dallas, Texas, to work for a Christian record company. Mom and Dad felt that my being far away from Jaye would possibly dissolve the relationship and allow me a chance to heal. I did end up moving to Texas and initially was able to rest and recover. However, before long, I started to yearn for Jaye's company.

As soon as he started coming to see me, things quickly went south. Once again, a dream job was in jeopardy because I missed too much work in order to be with him. My parents got wind of the situation and made a decision once and for all to cut me off from any financial support. They told me that they were not going to stand by for even one more day and watch me—let alone help me—destroy my life.

The problem was . . . I couldn't pull it together.

Living on a constant roller coaster with Jaye was taking its toll on my emotions as well as my body. Nothing about the relationship was right, and I knew it. The fact that he didn't take care of me the way I thought I should be taken care of was a frustration that I suppressed every day. Even if he couldn't handle looking after us, I wished he would at least talk to me about it.

And *marriage*. He never brought up the idea of marriage, but I was okay with that. Deep down, I just knew that it would never happen. Time after time, I told myself, *Walk away, Chrissy*, but I just couldn't. It wasn't an option because of how I felt inside: hopelessly, emotionally attached since the first day I gave my body to him. And there wasn't any reason for me to believe that I wouldn't be this way for the rest of my life. It compelled me to do anything and everything to be near him all the time, despite the cost. I couldn't necessarily say he felt the same deep connection with me, but it didn't matter.

Feeling trapped in the relationship was even worse when the bottom kept falling out—which happened once again. I was terminated from my job in Dallas. But this time, something snapped inside me. Between losing my job, losing my parents' support, and Jaye going back to New York, I reached my breaking point. I loathed myself so much that thoughts of suicide started to cross my mind.

While the baby was fast asleep, I would sprawl out on the floor, beating the ground with my fists, yelling at God for allowing this to happen. I wondered how I had become like the people my dad would try to help when I was a little girl—like the man whose tears were running down his face as my dad pleaded with him. At the time, I never understood why he cried, but what I had *wondered* then I fully *understood* now. He cried because he couldn't get free. Now there seemed to be no way out for me either.

I wanted so badly to go back to my childhood, hang on to Daddy's hand, and know that I was perfectly safe. But I was too far gone now. It wasn't that I didn't miss the love and comfort of my old world—I craved it. Only now that need was being snuffed out by the impossibility of my current circumstances that were killing me. And no matter how much it crushed me to have my baby in this pit with me, I couldn't see any rope in sight to pull us out.

Regardless of what I was going through, without my parents' financial support I couldn't make it. And since I had burned every bridge with all the people who had tried to help me in the past, I couldn't think of who to call for help. For now, I just needed to get back to New York, so I racked my brain trying to think of who I knew who would be willing to come to my aid. Then Lorna came to mind.

Lorna would do just about anything for me! I thought. *She loves me like her own daughter.* Plus, if anybody would understand what it was like raising a daughter on her own, she would. I picked up the phone and dialed. If nothing else, it was at least worth a try. My anxiety vanished when I heard her voice. She hadn't changed one bit, and her joyful greeting brought me back to a time when I was unapologetically adored.

As we talked for a few minutes, I could tell that she wasn't concerned about what had happened or even what was going on. Lorna just wanted to see me as soon as she could.

"Baby, call me back in a few hours," she said. "I'll need to take care of something first and then we will work it out, okay?"

After a couple of hopeful hours, I called her, and she told me that if I could just get back to New York, she'd be waiting for me at the airport. As I hung up the phone, I let out such a sigh of relief. *This could be the best situation . . . a safe and secure place for me and the baby and, even greater, Lorna might just accept Jaye and even welcome him into her home.*

A mass of cars and SUVs were jockeying for position alongside the arrivals pickup curb at LaGuardia Airport when I stepped outside the terminal. The cold November wind was piercing, making Susie burrow her cold nose into my neck. I scanned the cars, looking for Lorna's green Chevy Malibu until finally I saw her inching her way past the double-parked cars and pulling up in front of us. She jumped out and ran around the car.

"Chrissy! It's so good to see you, honey!" Her embrace felt like the warmest blanket as she wrapped her arms tightly around me and my daughter. Susie squirmed between us, trying to get a look at the unfamiliar face.

Lorna's eyes were filled with tears as she stroked my face. "My pretty girl. Thank God . . . He brought you to me. Come, let's get you and this precious one out of the cold."

After getting settled in the car, we began the ride back to her home.

"Lorna, thank you so much for doing this for me. I don't know what to say."

While holding the wheel with her left hand, she reached over and patted my leg just like she used to do. "Never mind, honey. You do know that I have been praying for you, right?"

"Yes, Lorna. I know you love me. There's so much I want to tell you. You probably don't know the baby's father. He was at the church for a short time. His name is Jaye. I really . . . um . . . hope you can meet him sometime soon." I pretended to look out the window as she turned onto the exit ramp, but I was really sneaking a few glances at her profile to gauge her reaction.

"Sure, I will. Listen, honey," her tone shifted. "I want you to know I called your father and told him that you contacted me. He did not agree with my decision to help you. But I asked him to allow me to care for you and the baby because it is what I feel God wants me to do. He said he would not try to stop me but insists that they will not help in any way." She paused for a moment and looked at me, as though waiting for a response.

As troubled as I was by that information, I decided to dismiss it. With the history my parents and I had, they were likely to give in sooner or later.

Turning my attention back to Lorna, I responded, "Again, this is really kind of you to take us in like this. Things have been very difficult for me and I just don't want the baby to—"

Before I could go any further, she jumped in. "Darlin'! We need to take good care of this little girl. *This baby* belongs to the Lord . . . and so do *you*. God hasn't changed His mind about how He feels for you, you know."

As Lorna said those words, everything became a blur to me. Pressing my forehead against the window, I thought, *How do I tell her that I believe what she's saying but can't break free of this thing?*

She must have sensed my stress because she gently ran her hand up and down my back. "So you must be really hungry. Are you ready to eat? I prepared your favorite! Curried chicken." She chuckled when she heard my excited gasp.

"I also have some things for the baby that I picked up."

"Oh, Lorna, you—"

"Now, never mind."

The uneasiness about my parents and even being back in Brooklyn started to subside. Being in that car with Lorna was the dose of joy that I needed so badly.

That evening I was treated like a princess—served a delicious meal and encouraged to take a long, hot bath. As I lay on the soft queen-size bed that Lorna said would now be mine, I snuggled under a blanket, wearing cozy pajamas that she was sweet enough to buy me. With my arms behind my head and surrounded by a mountain of pillows, I studied the room, enjoying the blissful comfort while Lorna fed the baby in the kitchen.

Our conversation in the car started to replay over and over in my head. *He did not agree with my decision to help you. He did not agree with my decision to help you.*

I knew how much Dad and Mom loved me and just couldn't

imagine him really meaning what he'd said. Sure, they were repeatedly disappointed by my decisions, but their love was too strong to keep someone from helping me. *I mean, what did I do to him that was so bad? I've been the one suffering, haven't I?* I continued to reason this out from my perspective. *Why can't they just accept this? I'm not twelve years old anymore. Why don't they treat me like an adult?*

The baby's voice traveling from the kitchen caught my attention and redirected my thoughts. The sounds she made were happy, almost as if she were saying, "Mommy, thank you for bringing me to a home."

Suddenly I envisioned my mom and dad sitting together, talking about their granddaughter and how badly they wanted to see her, to hold her. Then my vision started to change, and I saw them talking about how badly they wanted to take her from me since she was helpless and probably being mistreated. I quickly jumped up and scurried out to the kitchen.

"Hey Lorna, I hate to bother you with a favor, especially with all you've already done, but would you mind if I borrow your car tomorrow? I just thought I would drive home and try to talk to my parents. Maybe we could work this out."

As Lorna looked up from the baby food jar in her hand, her brow wrinkled. "Umm . . . I don't know if you should"—she shook her head, about to explain—"because . . ." She exhaled a resigned sigh, followed by a firm, "Okay. You can use the car."

"Oh, thank you so much!" I exclaimed and returned to the cozy bedroom. I slept so peacefully that night with a full stomach, thrilled that my baby was finally sleeping in a real crib across the room.

The Brooklyn-Queens Expressway was moving unusually well for a weekday morning as I zigzagged between cars, anxious to get to Queens. Reminiscing along the route back home wasn't at all what I expected it to be. A mixture of nervous excitement and stomach-churning dread began to build with each passing mile. It made me feel nearly sick, thinking about all the times I snuck out to go into the city, stealing my parents' credit cards and lying about who I was with.

But then I thought about my baby in the car seat behind me, dressed so beautifully in a fancy outfit that Lorna had bought for her. Her hair was combed and I had put a lace band with a bow around her tiny head. *Their hearts are going to melt when they see her. She is undoubtedly the ticket to win them over again. Surely they couldn't let me go back to Lorna's once they meet her.*

Envisioning what it would be like to live at home again, I thought, *They probably won't have me and the baby sleep down in the basement. The bedroom up in the attic is so bright, with plenty of space for a crib to go next to my bed. Then again, they may just want to put the baby in the room next to them so that they can tend to her during the night for me. Regardless, once they're with her, they are going to absolutely fall in love, and I'll just reap the benefits.*

My brain felt as though it were in a tennis match, bouncing back and forth, barraged by old memories that held me hostage for the rest of the ride. I cringed at everything I remembered that had happened between Brooklyn and Queens, all of which were driven by my destructive obsession.

Driving into the neighborhood, I was struck by a flood of warm memories. Images of my old, safe, love-filled world made me smile as I turned onto our street. The houses along the way were decorated with symbols of Thanksgiving—Indian corn, cornstalks, wooden painted turkeys—and multicolored leaves were blowing in the wind. I took a quick look at myself in the rearview mirror, pleased with the extra attention I'd paid putting myself and the baby together. The last thing I wanted was to give them the impression that my life choices had made me worn down and ragged.

Pulling the car into the driveway, I just stared up at the house. It felt like an eternity since I had last been there. With a nervous elation, I jumped out and rushed around to get the baby out of the car seat. As I pulled the hood of the little coat over her head and went to zip it up, the zipper caught in her dress. I leaned over to get a closer look and slid the zipper back in place, feeling little hands touching my cheek. Lifting Susie from the seat, I kissed her soft face.

The front of the house looked so beautiful with brightly colored mums in large planters framing the stairs leading to the doorway. Before I walked up the steps, I stopped and pointed them out to the baby and leaned over to let her touch them. Pulling open the screen with one hand, I rang the bell with the other, balancing Susie in one arm. As I waited, I peeked in the side window to see if Mom had put up the Christmas tree yet. *I wonder who they've invited for Thanksgiving dinner next week?*

Ringing the bell a few times with no answer, I looked back at the cars sitting in the driveway. *That's weird. Everyone's home.* I switched Susie to my other arm and onto my hip and knocked hard on the door. I waited, then I rang the doorbell a couple more times.

I was getting tired of standing there, so I slowly turned to go back down the steps.

What are they doing that they don't hear the bell?

Halfway down the front steps, I froze.

Wait a minute. They *did* hear the bell.

Suddenly, I could barely stand. It was as if a violent tornado was bearing down on me and knocking me off my feet.

My parents were turning me away.

All the blood I had in my body seemed to rush to my feet within seconds. I held on to the railing with the baby hanging off my hip, shaken to the core. Overcome by an embarrassment I had never experienced before, I walked back down the driveway to the car. If they were looking at me through the window, there was no way I was going to let them see me break down. Though the shock was absolutely crippling, I pretended to be okay.

When I got inside the car, it took everything I had to keep from unraveling. *Get it together, Chrissy. You can get through this.* Closing my eyes and clenching my teeth, I held the steering wheel with a death grip. I took several deep breaths to calm down, then I began to rummage through my purse frantically to find my keys so I could get out of there.

I turned the key in the ignition, and the emotions I held in check began to escape in whimper-like cries as I looked over my shoulder to check if the driveway was clear. Just as I began to back up the car, a *tap-tap-tap* on the window startled me and my heart jumped into my throat. I threw the car into park and rolled down the passenger side window so my mom could lean in.

Her face was completely blank, and she said in a cool voice, "Where's the baby?"

I stared at my mom, paralyzed by the shock of what had happened at the front door and now seeing her. "In the backseat," I said in a small voice.

Without hesitating, Mom opened the back door and scooted in as close as she could to the baby.

Shifting in my seat, I caught the softening of her countenance as love filled her eyes. She held the baby's fingers and whispered, "Hi. Hi, sweetheart."

Her voice began to break. "You're so precious, honey. I love you." I felt a dagger go through me when I saw her showing such tender affection to my daughter, the same tenderness that had once been showered on me. Mom didn't address me at all.

Finally I said with a slightly agitated tone, "Mom, what happened? Why didn't you open the door?"

Without looking at me, she answered with the same cool tone. "Chrissy, your dad is done."

Her words barely registered when I saw her lean in close to the baby's face and take a deep breath, almost as if she was taking in Susie's baby scent while kissing her gently on the face. After a moment, she leaned back, straightened up, and with a distant, fixed stare said, "And I'm done too. You're not using this precious baby to manipulate us."

In a heartbeat, my mom was gone, heading toward the house. As she disappeared inside, I felt like my heart had been ripped open. I couldn't believe she had walked away from us.

CHAPTER

24

THE SOUND OF CHRISTIAN MUSIC slipping under the door from the kitchen was fraying my nerves as I paced the bedroom floor. I was in a frenzy, almost hysterical. I wouldn't have made it if Lorna hadn't taken the baby from my arms when I walked in from that unbearable ride home. The expression on my mother's face—I couldn't shake it. My dad unwilling to see me was more than I could ever bear.

This can't be for real, I thought as my gaze roamed wildly around the room. Hurt, angry, and devastated by my life, I wanted to grab the glass vanity set on the dresser and smash it into a million pieces. The pressure from everything began to build up, and it seemed the only way to release it would be to destroy something. The music on the other side of the wall was getting louder as Lorna was singing along.

Something in me began to unravel as I replayed the sound track that wouldn't stop taunting me: the eerie sound of the doorbell ringing over and over, the broken tone of my mother's voice as she whispered to the baby in the backseat, my wailing on the way back to Lorna's. With each step I took across the bedroom floor, I could feel the life seeping out of me, and a despair deeper than I had ever known began to set in.

In an attempt to distract myself from the oppressive chaos in my mind, I went to the corner of the room, picked up some of the baby's clothes from the laundry basket, and began to fold them. I couldn't stop my hands from trembling as I threw Susie's pink romper on the bed and walked back to the dresser determined to pull myself together and get through the rest of the night. I stopped in front of my reflection in the mirror and heard that old familiar voice. *You've become such a letdown of a person. You're such a letdown that even your parents don't want you.* Standing there like a cornered animal, I had no choice but to listen.

My eyes flooded with tears that began to run down and fall on the dresser. As I stared in the mirror, all I could see was a waste of a life. My parents were right, yet I didn't see any chance of my changing or getting free from my way of thinking. I was who I was now, and I hated that person.

As I looked away, my eyes spied the clock radio sitting beside the bed, offering an escape. Rushing over to it, I fumbled with the dial, trying to turn it on as quickly as possible so I could drown out the cries that were coming from deep within my bleeding heart. I turned it to the maximum volume, lay down on the bed, and curled up into a fetal position, wanting nothing more than to make myself small enough to disappear. Groan-like sobs continued to pour out as I rocked myself like a child seeking comfort. Beneath the blaring music my voice cried out, "Help my heart! Somebody please . . . help my heart!"

The weeks that followed were nearly unbearable. It felt as though something snapped inside of me, making me ultra-sensitive and ultranervous all the time. The holidays going by without contact with my family made things even worse. I guess I should have been happier, given the fact that Lorna allowed Jaye to come visit the baby. There were times he'd come and the two of us would sit with Susie in the living room, appearing to be a family, yet I knew it was all fake. There was no way of knowing where Jaye stood with me. He was there, yet I didn't know if he was really *there*.

At times I wondered if Lorna was letting him come in an effort to secretly torment me, so that I would wake up and see my reality. *I knew my reality.* I was a worn-down, tired girl with a baby, desperate for this man for whom I had given up everything.

Lorna went to church a few nights a week—for prayer meeting and for choir practice—and I would sometimes sneak Jaye in. But even then I felt very vulnerable and fragile. I hated that I was lying to Lorna just as I had lied to my parents. But as weary as my heart was, I couldn't let go of that need to feel good enough for him.

It was on a Tuesday night in February when I heard Lorna coming down the hall as I was rinsing shampoo out of Susie's hair.

She poked her head into the bathroom. "I'm heading to the prayer meeting now, honey."

I looked back at her while leaning over the tub. "Okay, Lorna," I said, smiling wistfully.

She immediately picked up on how low my spirits were. "Everything okay, Chrissy? Do you want me to stay and help you get the baby to bed?"

I reached to pull out the drain stopper while thinking about calling Jaye. "Uh, thanks, Lorna, but I'll be okay."

I couldn't miss her concerned sigh as she walked back through the hallway to the front door. "Don't forget that there's more food on the stove," she called out as the door shut behind her.

I grabbed a towel. *Jaye needs to get here within the hour if we're going to be alone.* Susie started squirming and I strained to lift her from the tub.

"It's okay, sweetie." I quickly dried her off with the towel and wrapped it around her as I headed for the living room to call him. The house felt so painfully empty that a gloom came over me. An oppressive sadness seemed to slow my steps and weigh me down. I sat on the corner of the couch. After a long moment of staring at the empty chairs around the living room, I shifted the baby on my lap, grabbed the receiver, and dialed. The phone rang but no one picked up. I dialed again. No answer.

A suffocating loneliness suddenly gripped me and I began to feel afraid. I laid the baby down on the sofa and started turning on every light in the house. It seemed that the only thing to do was to put Susie to bed and go to bed myself. Since I knew I wasn't going to fall asleep, I checked in Lorna's medicine cabinet for any kind of sedative to help knock me out, but there was nothing.

When I finally got Susie settled in the crib, I put on my pajamas and cracked the door open a bit so that the light from the living room would permeate the darkness in the bedroom. Pulling the blankets back, I crawled to the center of the bed and adjusted the pillows, hoping I could shut off my brain and fall asleep. As I lay there in the stillness of the night with my baby across the room, I wished I could escape from all the tormenting emotions that I was drowning in; I didn't want to think, feel, or live anymore. Closing my eyes, I started to let out a tearless cry when suddenly I felt something strange in the room; the atmosphere had changed.

I opened my eyes slowly, not sure of what was going on, when I saw it at the foot of my bed—a pitch-black shadowy form. Even though I couldn't clearly make out a face, it felt nasty and menacing. I was arrested by what I was seeing, strangely unafraid, an observer who just kept watching. As real as that gruesome figure was, another one appeared—a cloud-like form just as visible, but this one was full of a beautiful bright light. It was as though I had become part of a crazy dream, yet I knew that I wasn't sleeping. I was very much awake.

All at once, the silence of the room was shattered when the repulsive figure started speaking to the luminous figure in a mocking voice. "I have her life," it said, pointing to me. Its next words were chilling. "And now, *she's* mine too." The shadowy form appeared to move slowly toward the baby's crib, large enough to cover it completely. My heart was jolted and forcefully seized by a strong instinct to protect my baby from the ominous cloud hovering over her. I wanted to jump up and fight for her with everything in me, but I couldn't move. In an instant, the darkness disappeared and the light faded away. Then the most unexpected sensation came over my entire being: peace. Sweet peace rested on me like a blanket and I fell asleep.

CHAPTER

25

THE NEXT MORNING I WOKE UP and sat in the middle of the bed, trying to shake off my sleepy fog. When I got to my feet, I felt an extreme sense of lightness. My heart was buoyant and my entire body was relaxed.

I called out loudly. "Lorna! Do you have a minute? Could you come here?" I needed her right away; this was so urgent that it couldn't wait.

"Good morning. What do you need?"

"Lorna, could we pray together right now? I just really need to pray."

I detected the surprise in her face but she quickly said, "Sure! Yes! We can pray."

"But Lorna, *I* want to lead us in prayer."

She reached over and took both my hands as I began to open my heart to God.

"Jesus, I thank You this morning for how good You've been to me . . . and . . ." I started to break down ". . . and my baby. I haven't deserved any of this . . . including being safe here at Lorna's house. Right now, I really need Your help. Please, Lord, help me to say good-bye to this relationship that I have not been able to let go of. I need Your strength because I can't do it on my own." While I was praying I felt a grace to yield my will like I had never felt before. "Thank You, Lord. Amen."

When I opened my eyes, Lorna had tears running down her cheeks. "Chrissy!" She reached over and grabbed my face, but seemed to be struggling for words. "I—I'm amazed!"

My questioning look prompted her to continue.

"This . . . I mean, you wanting to pray . . . was because of last night."

How does she know what happened to me last night?

"We were in the prayer meeting, like every Tuesday," Lorna continued, "but something incredible happened." She became even more animated now. "It happened at the prayer meeting!"

"What happened?" I asked, getting more confused.

She started rushing the words. "It was just that somebody gave your dad a note! He told the people that someone had just handed him a note and he felt that he was supposed to share it. It said: 'Tonight is Chrissy's night.'

"Chrissy, he read it almost like he knew *something* was going to happen. When we joined hands all over the building, the people started to pray. But they didn't just pray, Chrissy . . ." She gripped my shoulders and gently shook me as if she needed me to hear what she was saying. "They have so much love for you in their hearts that they were crying out at the top of their voices.

Girl, they were praying . . . they were shouting . . . they were making a loud noise up to heaven for you. The people cried out, 'God! Help her!' It just wouldn't stop, Chrissy! It went on a long time until we felt like we had broken through in prayer."

I stood there, stunned by everything she said. "Lorna, I don't know what happened," I said as I dropped my face into my hands and began to weep. Lifting my head to look at her, I said, "Something's changed! I feel different today. I just feel different. Last night after you left and I was getting the baby ready for bed . . . I can't even explain . . . it was such a deep misery. It's like I plummeted into a dark pit and wished I could end it all. Lorna, I looked through your medicine cabinet, and if there had been something that would have put me to sleep forever, I would have taken it. But there wasn't. When I got in bed, the strangest thing happened. A dark figure and a light figure appeared at the foot of my bed. I could see them! The dark one said I was his and that my baby would be his too."

I stopped to catch my breath, then went on. "I know I should have been afraid when the darkness moved toward the baby's crib. But I didn't feel any fear at all because instantly, the figures disappeared and peace flooded the room." As Lorna and I stood there looking at each other, I could sense God's sweet presence all around us.

After Lorna left for work, I puttered around the house with Susie, tidying up and getting everything ready for her feedings. The same calmness I had experienced in my heart the night before lingered throughout the day. It was indescribable. I couldn't help but keep thinking, *Did something happen to me when they were praying for me last night?* Knowing what I knew about God and having grown up seeing with my own eyes what God can do, I had to wonder: *Could I finally be free?* It almost didn't seem possible because of how long I had been in this struggle, adapted to living this way—so tired and worn, so driven and obsessed. Unable to keep promises to do the right thing. Controlled only by what *I* felt *I* needed. I just knew that I had no strength to try anymore.

While I was washing the dishes, God's gentle voice spoke to my heart. "You can do this, Chrissy, because I am going to help you." The voice was so real and reassuring that in that moment, I felt a courage I had never known before. It was as if something outside of me was pushing me to pick up the phone. The last of the dishes could wait a little longer.

I pulled up a kitchen chair next to the phone. When I dialed his number, my mind was clear. More important, I wasn't anxious at all.

"Hello?"

"Hello, Jaye. It's me. Do you have a few minutes?"

"Sure. What's up?"

"I need to talk to you about our relationship." Without going into detail about what I had experienced, I simply told him that I didn't want to live anymore the way I'd been living.

"For right now I don't think we should be together," I said. "Jaye, I don't know what the future holds, and I'm not putting this on you at all. It's really about what's going on inside of me. I've been in a really bad place."

I knew as I was talking that he had heard this all before and was probably tired of the back and forth too. But he had to notice that my voice was firm and not frazzled, that it sounded like there was a harmony in me rather than ramblings that made no sense.

"I don't want us to be apart, but I know it's the right thing for now. We can make arrangements for you to see the baby, if that sounds good."

"Okay, that's fine." I couldn't read anything in his response as we hung up.

Sitting at the empty kitchen table, I didn't crumple in a heap of tears. So many times before, I had wanted to end our relationship, yet I never could. But now I felt a strength flowing through me to do what had always seemed impossible. What I had wondered just a few minutes ago, I was sure of now: God was helping me and I knew I wasn't alone.

An overcast muted-gray sky stretched out over the snow-covered trees lining the street leading to my parents' house. The tires of the car crunched and slid on the layer of fresh snow that blanketed the driveway. A brisk wind blew outside the car, swirling the snow off the branches and onto the windshield. I turned off the car and sat in the silence. The fresh snowfall had softened the bare branches and hard edge of winter. Everything looked so bright and new around me. It was exactly how I felt inside.

With my hands still gripping the steering wheel, I stared up at the house and remembered the agony I felt the last time I was there. Flashes from that day replayed in my mind, and as the images rolled, strong doubt began to creep up on me. I was tempted to think that my parents would turn me away once again, since the ugly voice had already started whispering, *You haven't changed. You know your parents shouldn't take you back. You'll always be* that *Chrissy.*

As quickly as the doubt came, a supernatural courage and strength took over and chased it away. Because of what I already knew God had done for me, I chose to believe that He *had* begun to change me. After all, He had helped me take the first step with the phone call to Jaye.

If there was one thing I knew for sure, it was that my parents were merciful and that it crushed them to see me hurting myself. I continued to stare at the door, thinking for the first time how hard it must have been for them to see me standing on the doorstep with their granddaughter and not being able to open the door. I sobbed at all of the pain I had caused them, momentarily carried away by an emotional tidal wave. My decisions had all been wrong; I was now convicted not because I felt forced by judgment but because I felt so sorry. Their front door represented everything I knew to be true.

Minutes later, I got out of the car with Susie in my arms and started up the walk, knowing that if I crossed that threshold I would be saying good-bye to my old life. Joy began to flood my whole being, like the joy I had as a little girl! I pressed the doorbell, and within seconds I heard the doorknob rattling. As I stood there I thought, *How can I convey in words how I feel at this moment? How will I make them understand what I believe God has done in my heart?*

The door opened, and there was Mom's face, framed by the storm door. It felt like time stood still. Our eyes met and instantly a huge smile spread across her face. As I stepped inside, I dropped my bag to the ground and wrapped my free arm around her, burying my face into her shoulder. "Mom, it's over," I said, my tears flowing once again.

She held me tight, her voice breaking. "I know it is, Chrissy."

After a long embrace, we pulled away to look at each other. She searched my face as I asked, "Where's Daddy?"

I could feel Mom's anticipation. "Let me go get him." When she ran up the stairs, I headed for the kitchen, the place that held so many memories. I stood looking out the window above the sink, bouncing the baby in my arms. The joy in my heart was so great I could barely absorb it. *I feel new! I feel different. I'm home again and I'm free.*

The sound of Dad's footsteps coming down the stairs sent an electrifying excitement through me. I heard him say, "Where is she?" At the sound of his voice, the little girl woke up in me again. He entered the room with my mom close behind.

I rushed forward, handing the baby to her, then fell on my knees in front of him.

"Daddy, I've sinned against God!" I sobbed, one shaky arm holding me up as my other hand gripped his pant leg. "I've sinned against myself." I looked up at my parents. "I've sinned against you and Mommy. Please forgive me." Without hesitating, Dad pulled me up from the floor and held me close as we cried together.

Moments later we sat together in the living room. I was still overcome by what had just happened in the kitchen. When I had arrived at my parents' house, I *knew* that I wasn't the same girl anymore and that God was doing a miracle. But being on that kitchen floor and confessing my sin out loud had been the most liberating thing I had ever done in my life. I heard Susie

Joy giggle. She was on her grandpa's lap, his eyes brimming with love and adoration for this baby he had just met. My mom sat watching as though it was Christmas morning and she had just opened the best gift ever.

Dad stood up and looked at me. His expression clearly indicated that the past was now behind us. "Well," he said, with a note of celebration in his voice. "Do you know what we are going to do this Sunday, Chrissy? We are going to dedicate my beautiful granddaughter to the Lord."

CHAPTER

26

THE FIRST FEW DAYS OF BEING HOME AGAIN were like being surrounded by a sweet comfort and warmth that had been long lost. In all of my running, I had never stopped to think about what I had been missing. Dad and Mom gave Susie and me the best room in the house, a sun-drenched room on the top floor with its own private bathroom. The sounds of my home were so pleasing to my senses, which had been worn and battered—giggles, doors opening and closing, and even the clattering of dinner dishes were soothing to me in a way that brought back what used to make me feel secure.

My parents treated me as though nothing had ever happened. They didn't make me feel like I was tainted or damaged goods by the way I had been living. Dad and Mom seemed to see no reason to bring up the past; it was like instantaneous forgiving and forgetting. And the baby coming into their lives—they were absolutely beside themselves with joy! Watching how much they loved Susie was unexpectedly fulfilling to me as a mom. I'd just stare at my parents as they kissed her over and over, while under my breath I was thanking God for His mercy to me.

If my parents ever proved to me that they were "the real deal" when it came to their *talk* matching their *walk*, it was in those first days of being home. Their full acceptance really helped me to look with courage at the big day awaiting me—Sunday. Seeing my parents offer me such love and grace gave me hope that just maybe the people at church would follow their lead and receive me as well.

The faint sound of the congregation singing floated into Dad's office when Mom walked in. "Jim, the service has started."

Lorna popped her head in. "Hi, Pastor. Hi, Carol. Can I help?"

"Oh yes, come on in." Mom took Susie out of Dad's arms. "Lorna, the dress is lovely! She looks so adorable. Thank you, as always." She handed the baby to Lorna and came over to where I was sitting on the couch. "How are you doing, Chris? Are you ready?" she asked tenderly.

"Yes, Mom. I'm doing good."

Dad chimed in, "Well then, let's go."

My parents walked on either side of me as we made our way through the lobby. I could hear that the service was well under way, and I could tell the church was going to be packed with people when I saw chairs being set up in the lobby for overflow. When one of the ushers we passed said hello to me, I immediately became nervous.

I took a deep breath, knowing that this day was inevitable and I had made up my mind not to run from it. Part of making things right was to face the people who loved me, even if it dredged up feelings of shame. I came down the side aisle with my head down, trying not to draw attention to myself, taking my reserved seat in the front row.

It was a surreal moment—here I was in the church I'd grown up in, a beloved pastor's daughter, now unmarried and with a baby in tow. Mom sat next to me, and out of the corner of my eye, I saw Lorna being escorted in with Susie. She sat down on the other side of me, with Susie on her lap. Mom and Lorna joined in with the ocean of voices surging forth to God, the sound I had missed so much.

There in the presence of God, I closed my eyes and started to open up my heart wide to Him. At that moment, the only words I could say were "thank You, thank You," over and over. Suddenly a tide of love washed over me as God drew near. I felt like I was getting the same hug of perfect love that I had experienced at that little prayer meeting on Atlantic Avenue when I was a child. I just knew God saw me as that same little girl . . . that even more important than my parents forgiving me, He forgave me. For the first time in my life, I just had to praise and worship Him. I was crying, and although I wanted to worship out loud like everyone else, there weren't really any words coming out . . . my heart was saying it all.

God loved me so much that He forgave me and gave me

another chance. I had turned my back on Him, but He didn't turn away from me. I thought about what Jesus did when He gave up His life on a cross for me—something I hadn't thought much about until now—and how He took those ugly sins I had committed on His own body and died for them. It was real now! I understood why He did it. Now I could come into His presence unashamedly because of the great price He paid for my sins.

All eyes could have been on me at that moment, but it didn't matter—my heart felt as though it would explode. I closed my eyes, drinking in the sound of voices surrounding me, feeling uninhibited for the first time since I was a little girl. I raised my right arm followed by my left, reaching up toward heaven. I was so overwhelmed by what God had done for me.

The wave upon wave of voices settled into an interlude of sweet-sounding worship as Dad walked to the pulpit and took the microphone. He motioned to Mom, who was holding Susie now, to pass her up to him.

Holding the baby next to his heart, Dad began, "Last Tuesday, if you were here, you'll remember that I received a note and read it to the church. The note said, 'Tonight is Chrissy's night.' At that time, I shared with you that we had somehow lost our daughter. She was far from God and was even away from our home. That night the sanctuary sounded like a labor room, as we all cried out to God for my daughter.

"Today I am so blessed to tell you that Chrissy's back! God answered our prayers! Not only is she back, but she brought a gift with her, and that gift is my granddaughter."

No sooner had he spoken that last word than a torrent of cheers erupted from the congregation. People jumped to their feet, shouting, whistling, and applauding.

"Listen, everyone," Dad continued, "today we are going to dedicate my granddaughter, Susie Joy, to the Lord. Chrissy, will you come up?" Standing at the altar surrounded by my family and friends, I bowed my head as Dad began to pray.

"Lord, we thank You." Then Dad's voice rose and he shouted, "WE PRAISE YOU, LORD! We give You *all* the glory and *all* the honor because *nothing is impossible* for You." I closed my eyes and it was as though heaven was singing over me right then.

I was overwhelmed by the way the church celebrated my return, especially since I had abandoned all of them. They kissed me, hugged me, and poured out their love, treating me like a princess. I was their little girl again, as though there had been no gap in time, and it felt amazing. The euphoria of that celebration was like a lingering perfume that stayed with me. My parents were so happy, and that had always been something that meant the world to me. But despite the joy and celebration, melancholy started to set in.

I woke up on Monday morning and felt sad for the first time since I had come home. I surely didn't want to dampen the joyful atmosphere in the house because my parents were elated that Susie and I were with them, and I was too. We were a family again, and everything was back to normal. Yet now I had to live as a single mom, and the reality of ending my relationship with Jaye began to hit me.

One night that week, while sitting at the dinner table, I had trouble hiding how low I was feeling. I tried my best to finish dinner, even though my stomach was churning. Dad reached over and put his hand on my arm. "Is everything okay, Chrissy?"

I debated whether to open up and share with my parents how I felt about my sobering reality but then decided to keep my feelings private for the time being. I didn't want to spoil anything so I gently pulled back. "I'm fine, Dad. Just a little tired."

My mom got up from the table and offered to give Susie a bath before bed so I could get some extra rest. But since she had been bathing her every night to help me out, I insisted on doing it myself.

My sadness transitioned to tension as I walked into the bathroom with the baby and closed the door behind me. I didn't like how I was feeling, and it was escalating with each second. Pulling Susie's shirt gently over her head and steadying her while I turned on the faucet, a current of negative thoughts rushed through me.

Suddenly I was assaulted by that accusatory voice in my mind that said, *You're worthless; you'll never be good enough.*

I muffled a whimper with my hand, covering my mouth to keep the sound from escaping the room. My mind had been so clear and I had been in such a good place! But hearing those things, I felt drawn back to the same obsessive feelings again.

I wish I knew where he was.

"Lord, please help me," I cried out, my plea camouflaged by the sound of the running water. "I need You to—" Before my desperate prayer even got out, I heard the cruel taunts getting nastier, telling me that I wasn't going to make it and that I was nothing but a fake. I broke down again, keeping one hand on

Susie as I roughly wiped the tears off my face and tried to get the baby's bath over.

Now going down the slippery slope in my mind that I knew I should resist, I began to think, *Maybe he's with someone else now. I just wish I could see him.* My heart was crying out to God for help, but my mind just wanted to call him. "I'm not going to make it unless You help me, God, and I really feel like sneaking out and calling him." I started to think of ways to get out of the house without my parents knowing.

Everything in me wanted to run.

CHAPTER

27

MY FACE WAS BURIED IN THE PILLOW as I slowly woke up and became aware of my surroundings. Squinting at the bright sunlight streaming through the windows, I pressed my face back into the pillow, struck by one thought: *I'm still here.* As I started to get my bearings, I had a flashback of the night before in the bathroom, sitting on the floor, crying. This was the first time I had stood up to temptation on my own. But God had heard my cries and He helped me!

As I lay in bed, I thought about how the church had prayed for me, and I knew that was the reason I was home. But last night, *my* prayers reached God. Although I hadn't been honest with my parents the night before when Dad asked me how I was doing, I was grateful that God answered my desperate prayer anyway. Today was a new day—and I was okay.

When I came downstairs, I found my parents in the kitchen. "Mom and Dad, can I talk with you?"

Mom turned around and Dad looked up from what he was reading, slipping off his glasses.

I sat on the edge of my chair and leaned on the table. "Last night, when you asked me if I was okay . . . the truth is, I wasn't. I'm so sorry, Dad, to have been dishonest, and I don't ever want to do that again. When I went upstairs, I felt I was being attacked in my mind, so strongly that I was tempted to run. I know that if I had just talked to you and Mom, you would have understood and would have prayed for me and talked me through it. God was merciful to me anyway, even though I don't understand it. I cried out to Him, and somehow I went to bed and slept peacefully."

As I was sharing with my parents, I noticed that their expressions seemed to show relief that I was finally opening up to them. "I want to start talking to you because when I keep things in the dark, I only end up being an open target."

Before they could even respond, I continued, "So I may as well talk to you about something else that's been on my mind a lot. I've been thinking about Jaye, and I want to do things right before you and before God. But I just want to know, if God did a miracle for me—and I know I'm different now—why can't He do a miracle for Jaye? Then we could be a family and Susie could have her daddy. I don't want to sneak around anymore, but you need to know that I do think about him often."

My dad looked at me tenderly. "Chrissy, all your mother and I want is God's plan for your life, and we know that God can do anything . . . not just in you, but in Jaye as well. The question is timing."

"If you really want our counsel, Chrissy," Dad said, "we feel that you should wait a year before having any contact with Jaye.

Mom and I are willing to arrange visits for Jaye to see Susie and will take care of the details. By the time you see him again, we will all know whether this is the right thing for you. If God is in this, we believe that time will tell, so let's give Jaye an opportunity to show that he can take care of you and the baby."

When they left the room, I sat alone, reeling at my dad's suggestion. *No contact with Jaye for a year!* The impact of those words was a blow to my heart as I began to imagine each day that stretched out between now and then. *I just can't do it!* I silently cried. The longer I sat there, the more I felt like the walls were closing in on me. I wanted to do the right thing, but *this* . . . it was too much.

In the few weeks that followed, as difficult as they were, I knew that I had a decision to make: I could either set myself under my parents' authority and listen to their advice for the first time in many years or I could do things my way. I knew, however, that left to myself, I could potentially ruin everything. My dad's counsel to refrain from contacting Jaye triggered my memories of the last few years. As I replayed them, the bad memories always outweighed the good, and I realized that more than anything, sadness had been my constant companion. As much as I wanted Jaye and me to be together again, I knew that I didn't want us to "be" like we were. The more I thought about it, the more I knew my parents were right: I needed time to heal, to learn to trust God and myself again, before diving back into a relationship.

Dad and Mom were clearly aware of the impact our conversation had on me, especially when Dad asked me to join him on a ministry trip that he was taking in a few weeks. I did end up going, and we had a great time together. But during the entire trip, I was there but I wasn't there. My mind was consumed and distracted by the *what-ifs* and *how-wills* of my life.

On the last night, Dad knocked on my hotel room door. "Honey, I have a present for you." He handed me a paper bag. Inside was a beautiful black leather Bible with my name engraved in gold on the bottom right-hand corner. Breathing in the new-leather smell, I opened it up. On the dedication page my sweet father had written:

> Presented to:
> *Chrissy*
> By:
> *Daddy*
> *Philippians 4:6*

Later that night, when I was in bed, I reached for the Bible and looked up the verse Dad had written on the first page. It read, "Don't worry about anything; instead, pray about everything. Tell God what you need, and thank him for all he has done." Even though I didn't feel better that instant, lying by myself in the quiet of the evening, I was strangely comforted by that verse.

Over the next few weeks, I made it my sole focus to put all my energies into being the best mom I could possibly be. My world was starting to feel narrow, though, since it was now composed of simply going to church and being home with the family. A growing desire to be more responsible by finding a job prompted me to approach my parents.

One morning at breakfast, I brought up the subject. "What do you think about me getting a job selling makeup or clothing, like at a department store, maybe in Manhattan? I know I'd be good at it, plus it would be commission based."

After sipping her coffee, Mom set down her mug, "Chris, we are totally fine with helping you out in this season. We want to take care of you and the baby right now. But if your heart is set on working, then we'd recommend you pursue something different. Maybe there's an office job available that is closer to home. What do you think?"

I took my mom's advice to heart. Just a few days after I applied at a nearby temp agency, they placed me in an office five minutes from the house. Every afternoon, I came home for lunch and was able to see Mom and the baby.

It wasn't easy being a single mom, going to work each day and trying to get into the routine tasks of life. Living in New York City was even harder—knowing Jaye was not only a phone call away but I could quickly find him with a trip into the city.

"Absolutely, sir, would you please hold? I will try that extension for you." The phone lines lit up as soon as I got back from my lunch break. I was so intent on directing the calls to where they needed to go, I barely noticed the steady stream of people heading to and from lunch.

Someone dropped an envelope in the in-box on my desk and motioned to get my attention. "Would you have FedEx pick this up before 3 p.m.?"

I nodded and continued to connect the flow of calls.

Sunlight filtered through the wall of windows about ten feet away from my desk and brightened the reception area, inviting people to engage in conversations and business away from their cubicles. I reached into my lower desk drawer to pull out the overnight delivery paperwork when a sound arrested me. Usually the music playing overhead blended into the general sounds that filled the reception area, but this time I could hear the familiar song clearly, one that I hadn't heard in a while. Without warning I became paralyzed, and a knot started forming in the pit of my stomach. The sultry melody created a haze around me that began to cloud my mind—the song tempting me, wrapping its notes around me, and gradually luring me back.

The voice in my head was so strong, as if someone were leaning over me, seductively whispering, "You *know* you want to be that girl he's singing about. You will *always* strive to be that girl . . . *won't* you? Why don't you leave now? You don't want to sit at this desk. You know exactly where to find him."

I started to plan what I would say to my parents, figuring out how I was going to get to Jaye's job in Manhattan and where I would wait, even if it was just to get a glimpse of him.

Wait a minute! No! What am I thinking?

I covered my face with both hands. "I don't want to think like that anymore," I whispered aloud. "I'm gonna destroy everything. God, I need Your help again . . . These voices . . . I'm so tired of the voices! Lord, please help me right now."

The flashing phone lines on the board snapped me back to my responsibilities.

"I'm sorry, Mr. Harris is not available. Would you like to be connected with his assistant? Hold please." Even while I was taking the calls, I was still trying to shake off the sense of attack I had just experienced. But as the last two hours of work went by, I experienced a wall of calmness surrounding me. This whole episode reminded me of something that I'd heard a preacher say when I was a kid: "When we walk with God, it's not that we stop fighting—it's just that we've now invited Him into the battle." Once again, I knew that I was going to be okay and was actually excited to get home to my family because I would walk through the door with another battle won.

On the drive home from work, I thought about my reaction to the song I had heard in the office. Over the last few years, I felt as though the music had vanished from my life. Music had always been inside me, but with all the running, the obsessing, and the stress, it had become more irritating than soothing. I had stopped playing records and tapes or listening to the radio because I connected it to so many unpleasant feelings inside. *Am I the only one who is affected by music this way or is it true for other girls too?* My heart had been so moved by the messages and promises of those songs, but in the end I was always let down. I tried so hard to live out what the lyrics told me I needed to be, yet the words left me feeling hopeless and empty. I began to think about the songs that rattled me inside because I wanted to be "that girl" for Jaye. My playlist needed to change once and for all to keep me from going back down that road again.

As soon as I got into the house, I knew what I had to do. There weren't any empty boxes around the house, so I grabbed some garbage bags. I scanned my closet, my suitcases, even my old bedroom in the basement, feeling a sense of urgency. I didn't want to do it, but I knew it had to be done once and for all. Once I started stuffing the first garbage bag, my actions became almost mechanical—efficient and quick. One by one, I crammed in my albums, to throw them all away. I tried not to look at the covers because I knew once I did, I would drown in a flood of memories. Emotionless, I labored through the daunting process until I got two-thirds of the way through the pile. Sting's album was on top of the almost-full bag. Tempted to pick it up and look through the song list to pull up every feeling, every experience with Jaye that was somehow tied to each song, I nearly gave in. But I tied the bag shut and resolved not to do it.

I started filling another bag. Placing the last album into the second trash bag, I stretched the black plastic edges and formed a tight knot. I slowly dragged the heavy bags up from the basement and out the back door to the trash cans, careful not to snag either of them. Trudging through the snow, I grunted as I lifted the first, then the second one into the metal can, and firmly closed the lid.

I started reading my Bible regularly, hoping to hear what God had to say about me as opposed to the voices that tried to torment me. I knew I needed a lifeline to get through this journey out of my mess. God did speak to me through His Word—He made promises to me that jumped off of the page, words that I clung to. I felt like I was getting closer and closer to Him with each day. Surprisingly, the closer I was to God, though, the more I felt the sting of my past and saw the debris of my life. It was as though He was shining light on everything.

For weeks I kept mulling over the past seven or so years of my life . . . all of the wasted time, all the lost opportunities, especially the way I had hurt my family. My heart ached when I considered how I had shamed them and how I took advantage of their resources—knowing that when I was a young teen I could have talked to my mom but didn't. A weight of regret bore down on me as I thought of my expulsion from Bible school and the incredible jobs I had forfeited. Most painful of all was recognizing the amount of time I had invested in a relationship that went nowhere.

I began to see that although I was home and God had set me free, I still needed healing on the inside. My heart . . . it felt like it was full of thorns—thorns that my mistakes had put there.

One Sunday morning at church, Mom gracefully walked across the platform when it was time for the choir to sing. I was sitting in the back of the sanctuary, wishing I could be incognito that day. As the intro to the song began, I knew it right away. The last time I'd heard the choir sing this song, I was in the congregation, concealing my pregnancy, my heart stone cold. Now the soloist walked up to the mic, closed her eyes, and sang:

Smile, make 'em think you're happy
Lie and say that things are fine
And hide that empty longing that you feel
Don't ever show it, just keep your heart concealed.

She was singing about me—the unhappy life I had lived. As she sang, I broke down so hard that the woman next to me put her arm around me and began praying. The song continued:

Why are the days so lonely?
I wonder where, where can a heart go free
And who will dry the tears that no one's seen?
There must be someone to share your silent dreams
Caught like a leaf in the wind
Lookin' for a friend, where can you turn?
Whisper the words of a prayer and you'll find Him there
Arms open wide, love in His eyes.

Jesus, He'll meet you where you are
Jesus, He heals your secret scars
All the love you're longing for is Jesus
The friend of a wounded heart.

God's sweet presence came over me in such a way that I felt as though I were the only one in that room. He was speaking directly to me as the song was being sung. I wept uncontrollably as I released every mistake I had ever made and every regret I carried.

At that moment I could almost feel God taking my heart into His gentle hands, and He began to pull out every thorn—one by one.

I love you Chrissy, He said. *You belong to Me now. It's over.*

The next morning, before leaving for work, I came up behind Mom while she was making breakfast and gave her a hug. "Mom, the choir really ministered to me yesterday. I meant to tell you that God used the song to touch me in a powerful way. I'd love to talk to you more about it later when I get home."

"Oh Chris, I'm so glad to hear that! And it's so interesting that you would bring up the choir this morning because I wanted to talk to you about it. I was wondering . . . do you feel ready to join?"

CHAPTER

28

JOIN THE CHOIR?

I don't want to join the choir.

"Really, Mom? Don't you think it would be better if I just start focusing on the piano? I mean, I think I'm more of a musician than a singer anyway."

Despite my reluctance, for some reason Mom was insistent that it was a good idea. So the following Friday night I sat in the alto section—the newest member of the Brooklyn Tabernacle Choir.

I was pretty uncomfortable being so visible in the choir loft, although I tried not to show it. As thankful as I was for being back at the church, my return drew enough attention, and I would have preferred to blend in for a while. But then I reminded myself that if I was going to follow my parents' counsel, I had to trust that they saw something I didn't see in all of this.

The choir members each had an assigned choir leader, sort of like an overseer, when it came to things like attendance and tardiness. Mom appointed them to help manage such a large choir. The person assigned to me was strict to begin with, and seemed to be even harder on me. I made up my mind to be faithful to my commitment, though, and was learning to follow through on something for the first time in a long time. I wasn't about to disappoint my mom, and as the weeks passed, I began to enjoy choir, truly in awe of how Mom did what she did. Watching from the inside now, I could see clearly God enabling and helping her.

Life felt so narrow. I felt such a squeeze sometimes with working as a receptionist, being in the choir, and taking care of Susie. Yes, I was learning how to be responsible, but being responsible didn't come naturally for me. And when I had free time, I made a conscious decision to limit my church friends to those who had a positive influence on me. I just couldn't afford to be pulled back in any way.

Weeks had gone by, and one evening when I was home alone with Susie and feeling a little sorry for myself, the phone rang.

"Hey Chris, it's Al. How are you?"

Cradling the receiver between my ear and my shoulder, I continued to prepare Susie's dinner as we talked. "I'm good, Al. How are things with you?"

Since I had been back, my good friend Al and I hadn't had much of a chance to catch up. I was glad to hear from him. We hadn't really talked since the day I had gone to his apartment.

"Everything's great. Hey, we haven't hung out in a while, and I was wondering if you'd like to take a ride with Jimmy and me to Rhode Island next Saturday."

"Wow, what for?"

"Well, I've been praying about going to Bible college, and when I talked to your dad, he told me that there was a school in Barrington, Rhode Island, called Zion Bible Institute that I should check out."

"Sure, let me see if my mom can babysit. I'd love to come with you guys."

Driving along I-95 through parts of the beautiful New England landscape with Al and Jimmy was a lot of fun. We laughed quite a bit and acted pretty silly, but it was cool to hear them talk about what God was doing in both of their lives. Along the way, we stopped to grab lunch and ate in the car; it felt good to get away from the city, even if it was just for a day.

When we arrived at the school entrance, we found lush green foliage blanketing the grounds that lined the winding driveway leading onto campus. A building resembling a castle stood out as a centerpiece—it was majestic; I hadn't anticipated the campus being so beautiful. Someone from the admissions office took the guys and me on a tour through the different buildings, while I half listened to all the questions Al asked about the school and how it operated.

We stopped outside one of the dormitories, where our guide began telling us some of the history of the school.

"Excuse me," I interrupted. "Do you accept students with children?"

She gave me a puzzled look. "No, we don't."

Why did I ask her that? I was embarrassed that I'd asked the question out of the blue, and dismissed the idea immediately.

Bible college was a bad memory, and the thought of leaving home didn't sit well with me, anyway. On our way out, Al stopped by the admissions office to pick up the paperwork for enrollment before we headed back to New York.

The next day was Sunday and I went about my usual routine: getting the baby and myself ready for church, singing in the choir for two of our three services, and preparing that night for work the next day. There was nothing that hinted this was going to be an unusual week . . . and then Wednesday came.

Sitting at my desk, I watched a slow stream of people moving around the reception area. The phone lines had died down to intermittent calls throughout the hour, so I decided to start filing the papers that had piled up in my in-box.

Halfway through the stack I felt kind of weird, almost as if I were in a dream. As I moved steadily through the pile, my heart started beating faster. All of a sudden, it was like God was nudging me and saying, "Chrissy, you're leaving." I felt it again, but this time the nudge was stronger: "Chrissy, you're going to Zion Bible Institute."

Confused, I thought that this was the strangest idea going through my mind. *How is that possible? I couldn't be there even if I wanted to because the tour guide said they don't accommodate children on campus.*

Once again the strong impression came. "And *I* am sending you there." My eyes shot up to the clock that hung on the wall in front of me: 12:20. Barely containing my excitement, I put my purse on the desk, eagerly waiting for my lunch break to begin in ten minutes. Then, racing home, I burst through the door, looking for both my parents.

"Dad!" I called down to his office. "Could you come up here for a minute?" Mom was sitting in the kitchen tending to the baby. They both sat down, obviously anxious about what I was going to say.

"This may sound crazy, but while I was at my desk this morning . . . it was as if God spoke to my heart."

Their eyes widened—they weren't used to hearing me talk this way.

"I had such a strong sense that God was saying I'd be going to the Bible college I visited last Saturday with Al and Jimmy . . . you know, Zion Bible Institute?"

"Yes, that's a great school," Dad said.

"Well, I'm just so confused because I know I can't be a student there with Susie, but what I experienced today was so real."

Dad's eyes met Mom's, and then he looked at me. "It could be that God is doing something here. It just so happens that I know the president, Ben Crandall, and his wife, Jeanne. Dr. Crandall married your mom and me. But not only that, Chrissy—he was the one who dedicated you to God when you were a baby. I have his number; let's call him right now."

As my dad walked to the wall phone in the kitchen and started dialing, I sat at the table with Mom, too nervous to even think about eating lunch. Dad stepped into another room with the phone, and I could barely make out what he was saying. The longer the conversation went on, the more I braced myself for this whole thing to be just a figment of my imagination.

When he finally came back into the kitchen, he was still

holding the phone, one hand covering the receiver. "Chrissy, Dr. Crandall and his wife want to talk to you." I reached out and took the receiver apprehensively as Dad handed it to me.

"Hello? Yes ma'am . . . yes . . . oh, wow . . . okay . . . y-yes sir, I will call you then. Thank you. God bless you, too. Good-bye."

"Dad! Did Dr. Crandall tell you?"

"Yes, Chrissy. He did," he said, smiling.

"Mom, you won't believe this. They want me to come for the fall semester. I'm not going there as a student—they want me to come on staff to direct the school choir!"

Dad reached for Mom's arm, just as excited as I was. "Jeanne had been praying for God to send someone to lead the choir, and when I called, she felt sure that Chrissy was the one. She got on the phone and began to praise God out loud for answering her prayers."

As everything began to sink in, the rush of emotions turned into hurried words that spilled out of my mouth. "But Mom, lead a choir? I've never led anything in my life! Dad, do they know that I had a baby? I mean—" My mind was racing, riddled with so many questions that circled back to one: *How could this be happening?*

"Chrissy, first . . . yes. They *do* know you have a baby. And second . . . they *didn't ask if you knew how to lead a choir.*" He looked deeply into my eyes, his voice catching. "Mom and I have always known that God's hand is on your life, and only He could have done this."

When I returned to the office, I picked up where I had left off with the filing, although it was difficult to concentrate on my work for the rest of the afternoon. I was still stunned by what had happened over lunch.

This has to be a mistake. I've been back for only a few months. How can this be? But they wouldn't have asked me unless they meant it! An excitement swelled in me that was different from anything I'd ever known. I had just spoken to people who were strangers to me and they were *choosing me* to do something that important—unbelievable! *This wasn't a favor to my parents. It was too big a job to be offered as a favor.*

I couldn't wipe the grin off my face as I answered the incoming calls. *God's eyes really are on me*, I thought. The fact that He would put it on their hearts to consider me to be a leader at the school after all that I had done was amazing. The past few weeks had been difficult as I tried to navigate this road out of my past. At times I felt almost as if I couldn't breathe, but now this single event and this sense of God's loving attention on me filled my heart with a hope that ran in so many directions that I couldn't understand it all.

The next three weeks passed quickly, and I gave my notice at work so I could concentrate on preparations to move to Rhode Island. As the time drew near, I had nervous butterflies. But it wasn't the same nervousness I had lived with for all the years when it seemed like I was constantly sneaking, worrying, and obsessing. Yes, I was stepping into the unknown, but it was a place where God was calling me and where I knew He would help me.

Finally, it was my last Friday at home before Susie and I left. As I packed some final boxes, I realized that tonight would also be my last choir practice. *I am really going to miss this.* Being part of the group had been an honor, but more than that I loved watching Mom in action, sharing her gift of music. It was so effortless, and yet as she led us, I could plainly see her complete dependence on God and her sensitivity to Him.

"See you later tonight, Mom," I said, carrying a half-filled box down the stairs.

"Okay, Chris." She stopped at the hallway mirror to put on some lipstick before heading out the door. "Since it's your last night with us, I'm going to have the choir pray for you."

"That would be great. I'd love that."

It was 9 p.m. and choir practice was wrapping up for the night. From my seat in the third row of the alto section, I looked at the other singers, cherishing this moment with them. So much joy and laughter rippled through the room, the typical response after an intense practice and learning an entire song.

Mom was off to the side, giving the band some last instructions for Sunday, then she walked back to her podium. She leaned on it and smiled, then began talking in her personable, relaxed way.

"Choir, as you all know, Chrissy has been singing with us for the last few months. Actually, Chrissy, would you come down here and stand next to me?" Mom's voice wavered slightly. I got up from my seat and joined her up front.

"Tonight, choir, I'm going to ask that you would join me in praying for her. God has opened a door for Chrissy. A wonderful Bible school in Rhode Island has asked her to come on staff and direct their choir." She paused for a moment.

"When Chrissy was away from the Lord, I was in a season of real discouragement, but God gave me a song."

As I looked at the side of Mom's face, I could see tears welling up in her eyes.

"That song carried me through the turmoil we were experiencing with Chrissy gone. God encouraged me with the words He gave me—'When my strength was all gone, when my heart had no song, . . . even then God was faithful to me.' God did a miracle in Chrissy's life and once again proved Himself to be so faithful."

A wave of applause started and spread across the choir.

"And now, Chrissy will be leaving us. Even before she was born, God had a plan for her life, and we believe that nothing can stop His plan!"

As the applause turned into worship, I stood there, reminded of how much I loved my world and these people—a church family who was truly authentic in their love for me and their passion for God.

"So Chrissy has never led a choir before, but we know that God has gifted and deposited things in her that she's not even aware of yet. Let's pray right now."

A stream of ladies came down from the choir loft. As the group encircled me and prayed, I was really touched by their confidence in me. Peeking through the tight huddle of faces, I noticed Lorna in the crowd, her face glistening from tears of joy.

Sending up cries to heaven, Mom began to pray. "Give her the courage to lead, Jesus. Give her a heart overflowing with worship. Let Your name always be lifted up through her life, Lord. We pray that You'll strengthen her for the days ahead.

Please protect our Chrissy and little Susie. And we will all rejoice when we hear about Your faithfulness once again."

It was a gorgeous August day in Barrington, Rhode Island, the afternoon I drove onto Zion Bible Institute's campus for the very first time as a staff member. The sprawling grounds were perfectly manicured, and flowers in full bloom were clinging to the last days of summer. I parked, stepped out of the car, and did a 360, taking in everything slowly, then got Susie out of her car seat. As I held her in my arms, I said, "Look at the beautiful place where God has brought us. This is our new home!"

I walked to the main entrance, carrying my precious daughter. Pulling the heavy doors open, we entered and immediately heard, "Chrissy? Welcome!" It was President Crandall and his wife, Jeanne, awaiting our arrival! Welcoming their embrace, I was amazed that they had come to meet us. They were as warm and gracious in person as they had been on the phone.

Over the next few weeks, my life took a turn that I would never have imagined. As I went around campus with Susie, attended the faculty orientations, and got things ready for the fall semester, no one looked at me as a person who was unworthy to be there; I was given honor and respect. I was overwhelmed by the love and faith that everyone had in me. The staff didn't merely take care of my needs—they lavished me with everything they could to make me comfortable, treating me as if they had just picked an all-star instead of a rookie. My office was located on the second floor of the "castle," one of the nicest offices on campus and with a lovely view.

Our apartment was not just any apartment, but a beautifully renovated one with brand-new everything. I loved how sun-drenched and cheerful it was, a happy haven for my little girl and me. One of the first things that Susie did when we walked in was to roll around on the fresh new carpet, giggling with delight. Everyone on campus was nuts about her and did more than I could ask to assist me.

The greatly anticipated day came—my first class. It was at 10 a.m. in the chapel, and I didn't know how many students I would have until I walked in the door. My stomach was in knots as I made my way across campus, greeting people I passed and praying the entire way. "I really don't know how to lead a choir, God, let alone be in charge of anything. I am depending on You to get me through this." The idea of a group looking to me as their leader was daunting.

Coming through the door, I found a handful of students who had arrived early. Someone stopped me and we chatted for a moment, enough time for others to filter in and take their seats. I checked my watch—it was time to begin. When I turned around and took my place at the front of the room, a group of about a hundred students smiled at me. I breathed another prayer. "God, if ever I've needed You, it's right now!"

I took a deep breath and stood straight. Mom wasn't there in person but she was definitely there in spirit. "Hello, everyone, and welcome to choir. First, I'm going to ask you to arrange yourselves in sections—sopranos on the right with the tenors in the middle and altos on the left."

After the commotion of everyone finding their places, the room got quiet. I introduced myself and opened my heart to the choir. I spent the entire practice teaching the parts, section by section, without sheet music, emulating the woman I had admired my entire life.

After we went through it a final time, I asked them to take their seats and then I tentatively walked across the stage, aware that everyone was watching me. Sitting on the bench, I paused . . . then my fingers touched the keys. With my eyes closed, I softly played "Amazing Grace" from the deepest part of my heart. As the notes reverberated, reaching the choir members, the atmosphere changed. A holy hush came over the students and I knew they were sensing my heart going up to God. When I opened my eyes, I saw several of them lift their hands and as I continued to play and began to sing, soon they were all joining in. I leaned closer to the mic in front of the piano . . .

I once was lost but now am found,
Was blind but now I see.

With voices soaring in beautiful harmony, my choir sang with such a force that it took my breath away.

That afternoon as I walked back to my apartment, I couldn't help but remember a few months earlier when my mom had said, "Chrissy, I think now is the right time for you to join the choir." and my quick response—"Really, Mom?" To think that unbeknownst to me, God was preparing me for this day, one of the most special days of my life.

It didn't take long for me to start feeling more comfortable in the classroom and less self-conscious around other staff members. A whole new world of friends opened up to me as others on staff embraced me, despite the fact that I was the youngest teacher there. It had been quite a while since I had laughed so hard. They accepted me at face value, and the closeness that I developed with this group of friends was a real gift to me.

Many times they'd arrive at my apartment after the day's classes were over, knock on the door, and someone would say, "Let's go, Chrissy! Are you coming with us?"

"Just a second. I have to finish getting ready."

"Don't dress up. We're all super hungry. Come on!"

I experienced such freedom to be open and honest, with no need to hide anything from the people I was with. *Is this what normal actually feels like?* I began to have an inkling of who I truly was and what my purpose was. I realized I didn't need to be anyone else but Chrissy; I was chosen by God, even with all of my imperfections and my failures.

I was so busy with everything at school that I didn't spend much time thinking about Jaye. When he did come to mind, I avoided going down my former trail of obsessive thoughts. Instead, I continued to be hopeful that during this time when we were apart, God was somehow working in Jaye's life too.

There were many days when I would linger after the all-campus chapel service, alone in a corner of the auditorium, and pour out my heart in prayer. "God, I've given You my life, and now I need You to do something really special for me and my daughter. I want my little girl to have a daddy who really loves You and wants to live a righteous life before You. Most of all, I want Your plan because it's proved to be best."

Because the Bible college was only three and a half hours from New York, I would come home on the weekends when I could, especially so my parents could be with Susie. Sometimes I would leave her with them for an extended time, and during a couple of those visits, when I was back at Zion, Jaye came to see Susie.

It was incredible how God was teaching me that other than being chosen by Him, nothing else mattered. As much as I wanted things to work out for Jaye and Susie and me to be a family, I knew if Jaye didn't change, I wasn't going with him. I had changed, and I wasn't going to settle for anything less than God's best; I was not going to compromise and jeopardize Susie's and my future. For the first time since I was thirteen years old, being *chosen* by a man was no longer an issue for me. All that mattered was that God had chosen me. I was getting stronger every day, resisting the pressure to believe the lies that had ruled my life and had always left me in turmoil, a pressure I had put on myself for seven years.

Susie and I were enjoying a relaxing but exciting Christmas break with my parents—it was so different from our first Christmas together when she and I were at Lorna's, with me trying to be as happy as possible. This time, there was so much activity at home and at church and I was loving every minute of it.

One evening after church, a staff member came up to me and said, "Your dad would like to see you in his office."

When I walked in, I was surprised to see my dad, my mom, and Al there.

"Please sit down," my dad said. "There's something I need to tell you."

I looked at the three of them as I sat on the couch next to Mom. I couldn't tell from anyone's expression what this meeting was about.

"Chris," Dad said as he leaned back in his chair, his brows knit with concern, "lately I've wondered what's been going on with Jaye because he hasn't been calling to arrange visits with Susie." He paused momentarily, as if he was considering very carefully the words he was about to say. "It's come to our attention that Jaye is in a relationship with someone else now. Chrissy, I'm so sorry that this has happened."

I looked at my dad, wanting to respond, but I couldn't get a word out. I saw that his heart was breaking to have to deliver this news—that he knew how I had hoped Jaye, Susie, and I would someday be together as a family. I'm sure that it was less than a minute that I sat there, although it seemed like an eternity. Finally, I stood up and said, "I gotta go."

Al stood as well and volunteered to drive me home.

I was glad that Al was with me, but on the slow walk to the car, we didn't talk—he gave me space. I cried but it was a cry of release, not anguish; for the most part, I was okay. God had prepared me for this outcome. It had been nine months since my dad had asked me not to contact Jaye, with three months left until our "reunion." I appreciated that my parents and Al had been as hopeful as I had been for Jaye to change, too, during these months. But now we had the answer; we all knew it was over for good. And even though it was hard to hear, at least the news came gently from my dad, someone I loved and trusted, whose support for me was unchanging. I was done waiting and wondering. I was ready to move on.

In January, Susie and I returned to Zion for the next semester. I was where I belonged, where God had called me, where I felt invigorated and had purpose. I couldn't turn back because now I had tasted genuine freedom in all aspects of my life and it had changed me into a different person. I believe my dad saw that difference when he gave me the news about Jaye. He knew I wasn't about to return to that crazy life I had lived; he knew I was in a good place, where I could handle the disappointment without caving in.

I had come to realize that when you step out of the darkness into the light in a genuine way, you finally understand what a pitiful life the darkness has offered you. Thanks to God, I had so much more going for me, so much to look forward to; His best was yet to come.

Not long after coming back, I approached President Crandall and his wife, Jeanne, about doing a special project with the Zion choir. I had a newfound self-confidence that compelled me to bring it up. With my lack of experience, I was surprised that the idea would even be considered, but I was honored when they responded enthusiastically. Not only was I following in my mom's footsteps as a choir director, but now I would have the opportunity to do what she had done numerous times with the Brooklyn Tabernacle Choir—record an album.

The entire process took about six months to complete, from choosing the songs, to learning the music, to the actual recording sessions. The final product wasn't going to be limited to just the family and friends of Zion, it was going to be sold in stores! When I finally held the brand-new album—*Jesus Is Everything*—by the Zion choir in my hands, I couldn't contain my excitement.

The Crandalls and I agreed that a concert debut in Boston would be a wonderful way to release the album. Notices circulated throughout churches in New England, announcing that the Zion choir would be singing at the historic Tremont Temple.

The big day was finally here. I arrived before the choir and walked into the sanctuary, stunned by its opulence. Burnished golden trim accented the red-velvet seats on the main floor and in the U-shaped balcony, as well as the choir seating on the platform. The organ's pipes—framed by a stunning, ornate latticework—rose up as a magnificent centerpiece. Sitting alone in the auditorium as the choir started to arrive backstage, I drank it all in. I would never have imagined I'd have the opportunity to be part of something like this.

A Bible verse that I had learned when I was young came to my mind: "Now unto him that is able to do exceeding abundantly above all that we ask or think." Ever since I was a little girl, I had always wondered what that verse would look like for me. Now I knew. I sat there reflecting not just on the miracle God had done *in* my life, but the miracle He was doing *with* my life. God amazed me.

Before long the doors were opened. Excited conversations filled the auditorium as the guests eagerly waited for the concert to begin. When the choir members filed onto the risers, the noise died down. We were ready.

I smiled at the choir, and their faces came alive with radiance. Out of the corner of my eye, I could see Dr. and Mrs. Crandall, seated in the front row with my parents. After the introduction to the song began, I lifted my arms high in the air and began directing. By the time we finished the first verse, it didn't feel like a concert to me anymore. It was if I were back at the first prayer meetings on Atlantic Avenue, worshiping and experiencing God's undeniable presence. Love for Him had been the powerful heartbeat of that little church, and now it was my heartbeat too.

My nerves disappeared and I was in awe, really understanding the meaning of the words we were singing. It was as if we had been ushered into a holy place, adding our voices to a heavenly choir. I sensed the power of God's Spirit taking over, a power that was sustained until the final song. The music that had vanished from my life had been restored. He had put a liberating melody in my heart; there was no doubt I was now the new girl in the new song.

MESSAGE FROM CHRISSY
TO YOU . . .

Sitting in a softly lit coffee shop a few miles from my home right now, I can almost hear the music and worship from that concert so many years ago. As I come to the end of my story, I am so excited to finally be able to talk to you. I wish we were face to face. Although I don't know your name, I have been praying for you. I've been praying not just because I love you but because of how precious you are to God.

It's not an accident that you read this story . . . whether someone gave it to you as a gift, or you purchased it yourself. I believe God wanted your attention. You see, this really isn't my story—it's God's story . . . of how He can step into a person's life and make a transformation so great that the person will never be the same again. It's amazing to think that God is the one who created us and He knew us before we even came into this world. He formed us even in the darkness of our mother's womb.

I don't know where this finds you today, but if you feel something gripping your heart right now, it's not the book. It's not me. It's God's Holy Spirit. He's reaching toward you and He's calling your name, wanting to draw close to you. Maybe you've been running for so long, trying so many different things, in and out of bad relationships, and you find yourself like I was . . . with a tired heart.

Jesus wants to enter your tired heart today, and He wants you to experience a love unlike anything you've ever known. His love is faithful, His love is unconditional, and His love tells you every day that you're good enough for Him. If you feel right now that this book was God's note to you—just like the note that was given to my dad at that Tuesday night prayer meeting—and you want to see a miracle happen in your life, I want you to pray with me. I'm going to start the prayer and you can finish it, but if it's at all possible, go someplace where you can be alone. I'll wait. Go now.

I'm going to start the prayer with you right now, and then I want you to finish it. Whether you are on your knees or sitting in a chair, I want you to talk to God out loud and tell Him how you're feeling, the same way I did when I prayed that morning with Lorna. It's okay to cry because God wants you to come to Him just the way you are. Pray with me . . .

Dear Jesus, I'm coming to you because I really need you right now. If you are real, please do a miracle for me just like You did for Chrissy. I invite You into my heart. I need You to come into my heart and . . .

I'm praising God right now because if you prayed that prayer, I just know that He's already doing far beyond what you could ever imagine. He loves you. Remember, nothing is impossible with God.

If you just prayed that prayer,
go to chrissytoledo.com for next steps.

ABOUT THE AUTHOR

Chrissy is joyfully married to Al Toledo, the friend who had been there for her all along. They have three children and lead the Chicago Tabernacle, a vibrant, multi-ethnic church on Chicago's north side. Chrissy is passionate about leading girls (of all ages) into freedom that can be found through a relationship with Christ.

ACKNOWLEDGMENTS

If the following people had not followed God's prompts to encourage me to write this book, I would not have had the courage to do it: Ashley Wiersma, Cynthia Wilson, Roslyn Jordan, Ann Spangler, and Jan Long Harris of Tyndale House Publishers.

Thank you to my Susie, Annie, and Tommy for your excitement that carried me. I'm so proud of who you are.

Thank you, Shelly Torres and all of the intercessors at Chicago Tabernacle, for "praying this in." I love you all.

Bonne Steffen, you were a breath of fresh air throughout the editing process. Clearly, God chose you, and you are wonderful.

Greatest thanks to Dawn, my dearest friend, for your creative input and for holding my hand the whole way. Florida, Kentucky, Bahamas, Chicago, moo shu chicken, Thai rice, moldy carpet, robes and slippers, #sisterly-love.

And to my husband, Al, who wiped my tears, and was okay with me sharing this story for the sake of even one girl finding freedom.

NOTES

PAGE 6

It was a painting of Jesus: Although the painting was commonly referred to as "Jesus at the United Nations," artist Harry Anderson actually titled this 1961 work the *Prince of Peace*, which you can view here: http://teensleuth.com/blog/?p=17266.

PAGE 13

'O come, let us adore Him, . . .': This beloved Christmas carol, "O Come, All Ye Faithful," is an eighteenth-century Latin hymn ("Adeste Fidelis") attributed to John Francis Wade (1711–1786) and translated by Frederick Oakeley (1802–1880) and others.

PAGE 16

Now I lay me down to sleep . . .: A classic eighteenth-century children's prayer that was included in *The New England Primer*, the first reading primer for the American colonies.

PAGES 23–24

"Bless the Lord, oh my soul,": "Bless His Holy Name" is a paraphrased version of Psalm 103:1-2 set to music by Andrae Crouch in 1973. Copyright © Bud John Songs, Inc. It is featured on the *His Best* album by the group Andrae Crouch and The Disciples, along with other recordings.

PAGE 36

It was getting to the end of the night's show: Happy Days was a popular television sitcom that ran from 1974 to 1984 on ABC. I am recalling the dialogue in this particular episode to the best of my memory as an eight-year-old.

PAGE 41

In everything, give Him thanks: Written by Lanny Wolfe. Copyright © 1978 Lanny Wolfe Music (administered by EMI Christian Music Publishing). This song was on the Brooklyn Tabernacle Choir's 1981 album *Giving Him Thanks*.

PAGE 49

"Look at Me, I'm Sandra Dee.": This song, written by Jim Jacobs and Warren Casey in 1977 for the 1978 film *Grease*, was sung by Stockard Channing. The sound track was released in April 1978 on the RSO/Polydor label, two months before the film premiered.

PAGE 58

my favorite song began to play: "You Give Good Love" was written by La Forrest "LaLa" Cope in 1984 and recorded by Whitney Houston as a lead single on her 1985 album titled *Whitney Houston*, released on the Arista Records label. Copyright © BMI ASCAP.

PAGE 59

Tell them for me, please, tell them for me: The song "Tell Them," written by singer/songwriter Andrae Crouch in 1975, was released on Andrae Crouch and The Disciples' *Take Me Back* album, which took top Grammy honors in the Soul Gospel Performance category that same year. Copyright © Bud John Songs, Inc.

PAGES 59–60

Prince's popular song: The song "Kiss," written by Prince Roger Nelson, was a 1986 single hit for Prince and The Revolution featured on the *Parade* album, released on the Paisley Park label. Kiss lyrics © Universal Music Publishing Group.

PAGE 67

You probably know the song he recorded: "Every Little Thing She Does Is Magic" was written by Gordon Matthew Sumner (otherwise known as Sting) and Ninne Olsson and released in 1981 as a single as well as on The Police's *Ghost in the Machine* album. Lyrics © Sony/ATV Music Publishing LLC.

PAGE 68

Jaye began reciting the lyrics: The song "King of Pain" was written by Gordon Matthew Sumner (Sting) and was on The Police's album *Synchronicity* released in 1983 on the A&M label. It was the final studio album for the group before lead singer, Sting, left to pursue a solo career. Lyrics © Sony/ATV Music Publishing LLC.

PAGE 89

Dad's good friend and special guest speaker, Nicky Cruz: Evangelist Nicky Cruz was a former New York City gang member whose life was transformed when a young pastor, David Wilkerson, told him about Jesus Christ. Their story became a bestselling book and subsequent film, *The Cross and the Switchblade*.

PAGE 130

I was trapped in this life . . .: These lyrics from "Moon over Bourbon Street" were written by Gordon Matthew Sumner (Sting), a song on his debut solo album, *The Dream of the Blue Turtles*, released in 1985 on the A&M label. Lyrics © Sony/ATV Music Publishing LLC.

PAGE 148

Jesus, He'll meet you where you are: This is part of the refrain of "Friend of a Wounded Heart," a song written by Wayne Watson and Claire D. Cloninger in 1987. Copyright © 1987 Material Music (admin. by Music Services)/Word Music, LLC. All rights reserved. ASCAP. Used by permission.

PAGE 180

registered me with WIC: WIC refers to the state's short-term Special Supplemental Nutrition Program for Women, Infants, and Children.

PAGE 232

"Don't worry about anything . . .": Philippians 4:6, NLT

PAGE 237

Smile, make 'em think you're happy: From "Friend of a Wounded Heart," by Wayne Watson and Claire D. Cloninger. Used by permission.

PAGE 238

Why are the days so lonely?: Ibid. Used by permission.

PAGE 252

I once was lost but now am found: From the first stanza of "Amazing Grace," written by John Newton in 1779.

PAGE 257

"Now unto him that is able to do exceeding abundantly . . .": Ephesians 3:20

Online Discussion *guide*

Take *your* Tyndale reading Experience *to the* Next Level

A FREE discussion guide for this book is available at bookclubhub.net, perfect for sparking conversations in your book group or for digging deeper into the text on your own.

www.bookclubhub.net

You'll also find free discussion guides for other Tyndale books, e-newsletters, e-mail devotionals, virtual book tours, and more!